SPEAKING FOR THE GENERATIONS

Volume 35

Sun Tracks

An American Indian Literary Series

Series editor

Ofelia Zepeda

Editorial Committee

Vine Deloria, Jr.

Larry Evers

Joy Harjo

N. Scott Momaday

Emory Sekaquaptewa

Leslie Marmon Silko

SPEAKING FOR THE GENERATIONS

 Native Writers on Writing

Edited by

SIMON J. ORTIZ

THE UNIVERSITY OF ARIZONA PRESS   TUCSON

The University of Arizona Press
© 1998 Simon Ortiz
Manufactured in the United States of America

10 09 08 07 06 05   8 7 6 5 4 3

Library of Congress Cataloging-in-Publication Data

Speaking for the generations : native writers on writing
/ edited by Simon J. Ortiz.
p. cm. — (Sun tracks ; v. 35)
ISBN 0-8165-1849-1 (alk. paper). —
ISBN 0-8165-1850-5 (pbk. : alk. paper)
1. American literature—Indian authors—History and
criticism—Theory, etc.   2. Authors, American—20th
century—Biography.   3. Authorship.   4. Indian
authors—United States—Biography.   5. Indians of
North America—Biography.
I. Ortiz, Simon J., 1941–   .   II. Series.
PS501.S85 vol. 35
[PS153.152]
810.8′0054 s—dc21
[810.9′897]   97-21107
[B]

"Interior and Exterior Landscapes: The Pueblo Migration Stories," by
Leslie Marmon Silko, was published in *Yellow Woman and a Beauty of
the Spirit,* Simon & Schuster, 1996. Permission to reprint granted by
the author and publisher.

For the elders of all our people,
the good grandmothers and grandfathers
who have lived and traveled this road before us

And for Kaa-chanih and Ihtsah-tyaanih and their children,
and all who are the grandchildren of the generations before them

 CONTENTS

INTRODUCTION

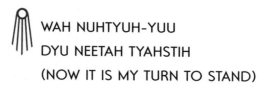 WAH NUHTYUH-YUU
DYU NEETAH TYAHSTIH
(NOW IT IS MY TURN TO STAND)

Simon J. Ortiz

Now it is my turn to stand. I'm rising to stand and speak in introduction of the essays in this volume. At Acoma Pueblo meetings, you formally announce your intention to speak, and when you do so respectfully, you are recognized for what you have to offer. You may then bring to the floor a topic or your views about a topic at hand.

Now, it is our turn to stand and speak: this is what the Native authors of the essays in this volume are saying. Some of the authors, like Leslie Marmon Silko, Jeannette C. Armstrong, Gloria Bird, Roberta J. Hill, Victor D. Montejo, Daniel David Moses, Elizabeth Woody, and myself are relatively, or at least modestly, well known, that is, regularly published novelists, poets, playwrights, essayists. A. A. Hedge Coke and Esther Belin, both younger and developing writers, have not yet published extensively, but certainly their voices warrant listening to closely. As representative voices of the Native people of the Americas, all the authors in this volume—novelists, poets, playwrights, and scholars, some of whom have also ventured into other artistic fields like painting, acting, and video and film production—have to be listened to when they say, "Now it is our turn to stand and speak."

They state this unequivocally and assertively. Since the 1960s, contemporary Native written expression has gained a wide and large audience. It has received serious critical attention—although

some critics have been somewhat uncertain and perhaps conde-
scending and too-liberal at times—and has earned considerable
recognition, but it still needs to be heard in every corner of the
Americas and beyond. About this there is no doubt.

Speaking for the sake of the land and the people means speaking for
the inextricable relationship and interconnection between them.
Land and people are interdependent. In fact, they are one and the
same essential matter of Existence. They cannot be separated and
delineated into singular entities. If anything is most vital, essential,
and absolutely important in Native cultural philosophy, it is this
concept of interdependence: the fact that without land there is no
life, and without a responsible social and cultural outlook by humans, no life-sustaining land is possible. I can hear the elders of
Acoma Pueblo and other Native elders saying, "We must live in the
manner our grandmothers and grandfathers lived. They were people who were thoughtful about the coming generations. They
were responsible in the way they lived so that the coming generations—we who are living today—would have a good life." Along
with this awareness, continually repeated as advice and counsel, is
the attendant thought to be pondered: we are living today only
because the generations before us—our ancestors—provided for us
by the manner of their responsible living.

   Human cultures and societies of all ethnicities, especially
those of predominantly Western orientation and persuasion, are
looking at indigenous peoples the world over. In 1994 the United
Nations declared that the decade be dedicated to the recognition of
indigenous peoples, their cultures, communities, lands, languages,
social systems, and governments, and their struggles for justice and
against oppression. Indian people—Native Americans—have especially been focused upon, primarily because they of all the world's

indigenous populations have steadfastly and unwaveringly continued their efforts to maintain and protect their lands, cultures, and communities of the Americas. They are admired and respected—although, also, too often envied and romanticized—for insisting on a concept of self that is absolutely tied to the interdependence of land and people.

The tradition of the oral narrative, expressed by the many different Native languages of the indigenous Americas, is at the core of this philosophy of interdependence. Traditional oral stories depict, assert, and confirm the natural evolvement—or the origin and emergence—of Native people from the boundless creative energy of the universe. It is articulated as an indigenous belief that is challenged, however, by a notion held by Euro-American culture that Indian people came to the Americas from elsewhere, namely Asia. Indian people have disputed this non-Indian contention, which to them is intended to demean and denigrate their indigenous identity by implying that their origin was elsewhere and away from their Native American world. Further, Indian people have seen this as an attempt to undermine their claims to the land they have always known as theirs and which is absolutely associated with their cultural identity.

Although "scientific" arguments are still posed by some historians, anthropologists, archaeologists, and Christian ideologues that Indian people are not native to the Americas, more and more plausible evidence shows that Indian people have been the human cultural inhabitants of these continents for tens of thousands of decades. Inevitably, and perhaps soon, evidence will substantiate the indigenous view that we have always lived here.

Acoma Pueblo people believe they came into Existence as a human culture and community at Shipapu, which they know as a sacred mythic place of origin. Shipapu and a belief in Shipapu, therefore and thereafter, is the mythic source of their Existence. Coming into Existence from a source like Shipapu is indisputably an assertion of their direct relationship with the creative spirit-force-dynamic of the earth. This belief obviously precedes the advent of European cultural civilization in the Americas, and as such it is a traditional concept of origin-emergence (or some similar version of it expressed as a belief-story) that all Indian people throughout the Americas share. The sense that we have always lived here is reiterated continually in oral narrative. The young are frequently reminded by their elders: these lands and waters and all elements of Creation are a part of you, and you are a part of them; you have a reciprocal relationship with them.

This belief is expressed time and time again in traditional song, ritual, prayer, and story, and in contemporary writing. Verbalizing, articulating, and practicing it in social and religious activities today is simply carrying on a traditional way of life that the oral narrative has expressed since the dawn of indigenous Native American humankind and its culture.

Today's Native novelists, poets, playwrights, essayists, songwriters, filmwriters, and others are simply continuing a tradition. Personally, I don't know if I ever "decided" to be a writer and poet, but I know I have felt it was important to participate in the act of helping to carry on the expression of a way of life that I believed in.

I grew up alongside the Rio de San Jose (a name given it by the Spanish colonizers, just like they also "gave" us Pueblo Indians most of our last names), which emerges from beneath the volcanic lava beds west of Deetzihyaamah (or McCartys, in English), a village north of Aacquh, the old pueblo. As Acoma people we have always believed the *chunah* (our Acoma name for it, which denotes the natural landscape feature of a water channel) was more than just a water source. It was more than just irrigation water for our corn, chili, and hay fields, and our orchards, more than just water for our households and for our livestock, and more than just the great native trout fishing stream that I knew as a boy. It was a life-giving water source that came eastward from the direction of Hee-shamih Quuti in the Zuni Mountains to the west and the Continental Divide, of which the mountains are a part, and the water in the chunah followed the same route the Shiwana did when they, as rain clouds, brought their sacred life-giving moisture to us.

Believing the chunah is more than a water source is an integral feature of an Acoma Pueblo belief that absolutely accepts—and therefore insists on the maintenance and continuance of—the reciprocal relationship that we as a human culture have with the natural environment in which we live. The life-giving water, then, has a cosmological characteristic that is knowable as the Shiwana with whom the people of Acoma Pueblo and other southwestern Pueblos have communication through traditional ritual and ceremonial activities that include song, dance, spiritual meditation, and oral narrative, which all affirm the concept of a reciprocal relationship with all things in Creation.

The water in the chunah, the land that the water nourishes and is nourished by, and all other life elements, items, features, and aspects of Creation make up what we know to be Existence. This is what I mean when I say that the chunah is more than just a water source, and as a writer this is what I try to make apparent in my writing because my own writing comes from a similar dynamic of reciprocity shared by the land, water, and human culture. And because modern-day American life has brought changes to the natural landscape such as the water in the chunah, as well as changes to the human cultural landscape of Acoma, inevitably I address those matters. I feel it is necessary to do so; there is no way to avoid that responsibility as a member of today's Native community.

It is necessary to speak on behalf of Native people and their homeland. Almost from the beginning time when I first began, more or less consciously, to know myself as a writer (after a period of not knowing exactly what I was doing, of course), it was important for me to express myself as an Indian. Of course, I also had self-questions and qualms about the extensive use of the English language and the Western cultural baggage that came with it. English was definitely a second language for me, since my first and native one was the Acoma language. I also knew that there were many Indian people who did not read, write, and speak in English—some preferring *not* to deal with the baggage. Yet I chose to be an Indian writer using the English language since that was the predominant one that Indian people faced.

Using the English language is a dilemma and pretty scary sometimes, because it means letting one's mind go willfully— although with soul and heart in shaky hand, literally—into the Western cultural and intellectual context, a condition and circumstance that one usually avoids at all costs on most occasions. Even though I believe I did not have many overt problems with it, learning to speak, read, and write in English was fraught with considerable tension for me. As a result, years later I admit I have felt uneasy and even disloyal at moments when I've found myself to be more verbally articulate in the English language than in my own native Acoma language. I have to honestly admit that there is a price to pay for selling your soul, if that's what has happened.

In any case, the dilemma not withstanding, there has never been any lack of topics to address, like the above chunah, for instance, alongside which I grew up. I loved that little stream, from which we would carry buckets of water to wash our clothes and to give to our chickens, rabbits, and pigs. The chunah is where I learned to swim, and the chunah is where we used to catch the best trout, and also catfish and suckers. Every memory I have of my Acoma childhood has in it the chunah two hundred yards north of our home in McCartys. But as I mentioned above, modern American life has wrought many changes. Over the past forty years I've seen the chunah change from a stream running full and vigorous in its channel to one flowing limply and weakly, and from being clear and clean to being gray and brackish. So, as a writer whose native landscape has changed, in some instances drastically and traumatically, I've focused on this change as a topic in most of my writings.

The United States of America is not a democracy in its relationship to Native people and their lands. It has never dealt with Indians fairly and equally. The nation's stated ideal of justice for all has never been upheld in its treatment of Indian people. Before the nation was established, English, French, and Spanish colonial settlement of the Americas was achieved as a conquest of land and people, so it followed that any future relations with Native lands and people would be determined by an ethic based on the idea that "the winner takes all." After its nationhood was established, the United States declared itself the winner in all respects; therefore Indians could be dealt with and treated in any way the winner wanted.

Although the story of the relationship between the U.S. society and government and Indian people is well known in some respects, it is not very well known in other ways. The concept of the interdependence of the land and people is not always at the forefront of discussions between Indians and non-Indians, and when Indian people do bring up the matter of land and people being inextricably bound together, the question is often shunted aside as "an Indian cultural matter." If it is not altogether dismissed, it is often regarded as beside the point or not directly pertinent. However, it has become increasingly necessary for contemporary human culture to turn its attention to this concept directly and to listen to those voices that speak for all the land and all the people. As an influence—in fact, as an essential element—in the development of my writing, my Native voice has come from the concept of the necessary and essential relationship of land and people, and it is my hope and wish that this voice will have Continuance as the land and people continue to have Existence.

I debated with myself seriously about using the terms *Native American, Native, First Nation, Indigenous, Indian,* and so forth, and decided to use—or give some weight to—the term *Native* in this introduction since it is helpful and pertinent in identifying as a whole the indigenous heritage of Native Canadian, Guatemalan, and U.S. writers in this volume whose peoples and cultures are *native* to this hemisphere and the lands now generally known as North, Central, and South America. Some of the writers identify themselves by their specific cultural and place names. For example, I identify myself as Acoma or Aacquhmeh (a person of the Acoma people) because I was born of the Acoma Pueblo people and my native cultural identity is Acoma. When I say I am from Acoma, I am speaking about my cultural identity, but I am also talking about the place where my native culture and community reside in New Mexico.

I also thought about the use of the term *tribe,* which is a common enough usage. On most occasions I try not to use it because I consider the term intentionally restrictive and exclusionary; it is part of the social and political beliefs and practices that categorize Native people into small units—villages, hamlets, settlements, indiscernible and anonymous bands, and minuscule tribal groups, so to speak. It reflects a Euro-American or Western historical and cultural attitude of domination, conquest, and control, and by categorizing them it excludes Native people from the general human population of the Americas.

There should be no confusion when the writers use their own culturally determined term or name for themselves as Native people, although an academic or technical argument might be posed by some people who prefer to see Natives strictly categorized, identified, and designated as Indians so that there would be no doubt about *that,* so to speak, in their terms. Nonetheless, the writers in this volume are speaking for themselves, their land, and their people as they speak for the generations. They speak for the continuing Existence of all life. Listen, they are speaking.

SPEAKING FOR THE GENERATIONS

INTERIOR AND EXTERIOR LANDSCAPES

 THE PUEBLO MIGRATION STORIES

Leslie Marmon Silko

From a High Arid Plateau in New Mexico

You see that, after a thing is dead, it dries up. It might take weeks or years, but eventually, if you touch the thing, it crumbles under your fingers. It goes back to dust. The soul of the thing has long since departed. With the plants and wild game the soul may have already been born back into bones and blood or thick green stalks and leaves. Nothing is wasted. What cannot be eaten by people or in some way used must then be left where other living creatures may benefit. What domestic animals or wild scavengers can't eat will be fed to the plants. The plants feed on the dust of these few remains.

The ancient Pueblo people buried the dead in vacant rooms or in partially collapsed rooms adjacent to the main living quarters. Sand and clay used to construct the roof make layers many inches deep once the roof has collapsed. The layers of sand and clay make for easy grave-digging. The vacant room fills with cast-off objects and debris. When a vacant room has filled deep enough, a shallow but adequate grave can be scooped in a far corner. Archaeologists have remarked over formal burials complete with elaborate funerary objects excavated in trash middens of abandoned rooms. But the rocks and adobe mortar of collapsed walls were valued by the ancient people. Because each rock had been carefully selected for size and shape, then chiseled to an even face. Even the pink clay adobe melting with each rainstorm had to prayed over, then dug and carried some distance. Corncobs and husks, the rinds and stalks and animal bones were not regarded as filth or garbage. The remains were merely resting at a midpoint in their journey back to dust. Human remains are not so different. They should rest with the bones and rinds where they all may benefit living creatures— small rodents and insects—until their return is completed. The remains of things—animals and plants, the clay and stones—were treated with respect, because for the ancient people all these things had spirit and being.[1]

The antelope merely consents to return home with the hunter. All phases of the hunt are conducted with love: the love the hunter and the people have for the Antelope People, and the love of the antelope who agree to give up their meat and blood so that human beings will not starve. Waste of meat or even the thoughtless handling of bones cooked bare will offend the antelope spirits. Next year the hunters will vainly search the dry plains for antelope. Thus, it is necessary to return carefully the bones and hair, and the stalks and leaves to the earth who first created them. The spirits remain close by. They do not leave us.

The dead become dust, and in this becoming they are once more joined with the Mother. The ancient Pueblo people called the earth the Mother Creator of all things in this world. Her sister, the Corn Mother, occasionally merges with her because all succulent green life arises out of the depths of the earth.

Rocks and clay are part of the Mother. They merge in various forms, but at some time before they were smaller particles of

Leslie Marmon Silko

great boulders. At a later time they may again become what they once were: dust.

A rock shares this fate with us and with animals and plants as well. A rock has being or spirit, although we may not understand it. The spirit may differ from the spirit we know in animals or plants or in ourselves. In the end we all originate from the depths of the earth. Perhaps this is how all beings share in the spirit of the Creator. We do not know.

From the Emergence Place

Pueblo potters, the creators of petroglyphs and oral narratives, never conceived of removing themselves from the earth and sky. So long as the human consciousness remains *within* the hills, canyons, cliffs, and the plants, clouds, and sky, the term *landscape,* as it has entered the English language, is misleading. "A portion of territory the eye can comprehend in a single view" does not correctly describe the relationship between the human being and his or her surroundings. This assumes the viewer is somehow *outside* or *separate from* the territory she or he surveys. Viewers are as much a part of the landscape as the boulders they stand on.

There is no high mesa or mountain peak where one can stand and not immediately be part of all that surrounds. Human identity is linked with all the elements of Creation through the clan; you might belong to the Sun Clan or the Lizard Clan or the Corn Clan or the Clay Clan.[2] Standing deep within the natural world, the ancient Pueblo understood the thing as it was—the squash blossom, grasshopper, or rabbit itself could never be created by the human hand. Ancient Pueblos took the modest view that the thing itself (the landscape) could not be improved upon. The ancients did not presume to tamper with what had already been created. Thus, *realism,* as we now recognize it in painting and sculpture, did not catch the imaginations of Pueblo people until recently.

The squash blossom itself is *one thing*: itself. So the ancient Pueblo potter abstracts what she saw to be the key elements of the squash blossom—the four symmetrical petals, with four symmetrical stamens in the center. These key elements, while suggesting the squash flower, also link it with the four cardinal directions. By representing only its intrinsic form, the squash flower is released from a limited meaning or restricted identity. Even in the most sophisticated abstract form, a squash flower or a cloud or a lightning bolt became intricately connected with a complex system of relationships which the ancient Pueblo people maintained with each other, and with the populous natural world they lived within. A bolt of lightning is itself, but at the same time it may mean much more. It may be a messenger of good fortune when summer rains are needed. It may deliver death, perhaps the result of manipulations by the Gunnadeyahs, destructive necromancers. Lightning may strike down an evildoer, or lightning may strike a person of good will. If the person survives, lightning endows him or her with heightened power.

Pictographs and petroglyphs of constellations or elk or antelope draw their magic in part from the process wherein the focus of all prayer and concentration is upon the thing itself, which, in its turn, guides the hunter's hand. Connection with the spirit dimensions requires a figure or form that is all-inclusive. A "lifelike" rendering of an elk is too restrictive. Only the elk *is* itself. A *realistic* rendering of an elk would be only one particular elk anyway. The purpose of the hunt rituals and magic is to make contact with *all* the spirits of the Elk.

The land, the sky, and all that is within them—the land-scape—includes human beings. Interrelationships in the Pueblo landscape are complex and fragile. The unpredictability of the weather, the aridity and harshness of much of the terrain in the high plateau country explain in large part the relentless attention the ancient Pueblo people gave to the sky and the earth around them. Survival depended upon harmony and cooperation not only among human beings, but also among all things—the animate and the less animate, since rocks and mountains were known on occasion to move.

The ancient Pueblos believed the Earth and the Sky were sisters (or sister and brother in the post-Christian version). As long as food-family relations are maintained, then the Sky will continue to bless her sister, the Earth, with rain, and the Earth's children will continue to survive. But the old stories recall incidents in which troublesome spirits or beings threaten the earth. In one story, a malicious *ka'tsina,* called the Gambler, seizes the Shiwana, or Rain-clouds, the Sun's beloved children.[3] The Shiwana are snared in magical power late one afternoon on a high mountaintop. The Gambler takes the Rainclouds to his mountain stronghold where he locks them in the north room of his house. What was his idea? The Shiwana were beyond value. They brought life to all things on earth. The Gambler wanted a big stake to wager in his games of chance. But such greed, even on the part of only one being, had the effect of threatening the survival of all life on earth. Sun Youth, aided by old Grandmother Spider, outsmarts the Gambler and the rigged game, and the Rainclouds are set free. The drought ends, and once more life thrives on earth.

Through the Stories We Hear Who We Are

All summer the people watch the west horizon, scanning the sky from south to north for rain clouds. Corn must have moisture at the time the tassels form. Otherwise pollination will be incomplete, and the ears will be stunted and shriveled. An inadequate harvest may bring disaster. Stories told at Hopi, Zuni, and at Acoma and Laguna describe drought and starvation as recently as 1900. Precipitation in west-central New Mexico averages fourteen inches annually. The western pueblos are located at altitudes over five thousand six hundred feet above sea level, where winter temperatures at night fall below freezing. Yet evidence of their presence in the high desert and plateau country goes back ten thousand years. The ancient Pueblo not only survived in this environment, but for many years they also thrived. In A.D. 1100 the people at Chaco Canyon had built cities with apartment buildings of stone five stories high.[4] Their sophistication as sky-watchers was surpassed only by Mayan and Inca astronomers. Yet this vast complex of knowledge and belief, amassed for thousands of years, was never recorded in writing.

Instead, the ancient Pueblo people depended upon collective memory through successive generations to maintain and transmit an entire culture, a worldview complete with proven strategies for survival. The oral narrative, or story, became the medium through which the complex of Pueblo knowledge and belief was maintained. Whatever the event or the subject, the ancient people perceived the world and themselves within that world as part of an ancient, continuous story composed of innumerable bundles of other stories.

The ancient Pueblo vision of the world was inclusive. The

impulse was to leave nothing out. Pueblo oral tradition necessarily embraced all levels of human experience. Otherwise, the collective knowledge and beliefs comprising ancient Pueblo culture would have been incomplete. Thus, stories about the Creation and Emergence of human beings and animals into this world continue to be retold each year for four days and four nights during the winter solstice. The *humma-hah* stories related events from the time long ago when human beings were still able to communicate with animals and other living things.[5] But beyond these two preceding categories, the Pueblo oral tradition knew no boundaries. Accounts of the appearance of the first Europeans (Spanish) in Pueblo country or of the tragic encounters between Pueblo people and Apache raiders were no more and no less important than stories about the biggest mule deer ever taken or adulterous couples surprised in cornfields and chicken coops. Whatever happened, the ancient people instinctively sorted events and details into a loose narrative structure. Everything became a story.

Traditionally everyone, from the youngest child to the oldest person, was expected to listen and be able to recall or tell a portion of, if only a small detail from, a narrative account or story. Thus, the remembering and the retelling were a communal process. Even if a key figure, an elder who knew much more than others, were to die unexpectedly, the system would remain intact. Through the efforts of a great many people, the community was able to piece together valuable accounts and crucial information that might otherwise have died with an individual.

Communal storytelling was a self-correcting process in which listeners were encouraged to speak up if they noted an important fact or detail omitted. The people were happy to listen to two or three different versions of the same event of the same *humma-hah* story. Even conflicting versions of an incident were welcomed for the entertainment they provided. Defenders of each version might joke and tease one another, but seldom were there any direct confrontations. Implicit in the Pueblo oral tradition was the awareness that loyalties, grudges, and kinship must always influence the narrator's choices as she emphasizes to listeners that this is the way *she* has always heard the story told. The ancient Pueblo people sought a communal truth, not an absolute truth. For them this truth lived somewhere within the web of differing versions, disputes over minor points, and outright contradictions tangling with old feuds and village rivalries.

A dinner-table conversation recalling a deer hunt forty years ago, when the largest mule deer ever was taken, inevitably stimulates similar memories in listeners. But hunting stories were not merely after-dinner entertainment. These accounts contained information of critical importance about the behavior and migration patterns of mule deer. Hunting stories carefully described key landmarks and locations of fresh water. Thus, a deer-hunt story might also serve as a map. Lost travelers, and lost piñon-nut gatherers, have been saved by sighting a rock formation they recognize only because they once heard a hunting story describing this rock formation.

The importance of cliff formations and water holes does not end with hunting stories. As offspring of the Mother Earth, the ancient Pueblo people could not conceive of themselves within a specific landscape, but location, or place, nearly always plays a central role in the Pueblo oral narratives. Indeed, stories are mostly frequently recalled as people are passing by a specific geographical feature or the exact location where a story took place. The precise date of the incident often is less important than the place or location of the happening. "Long, long ago," "a long time ago," "not too long ago," and "recently" are usually how stories are classified in terms of time. But the places where the stories occur are precisely located, and prominent geographical details recalled, even if the landscape is well known to listeners, often because the turning point in the narrative involved a peculiarity of the special quality of a rock or tree or plant found only at that place. Thus, in the case of many of the Pueblo narratives, it is impossible to determine which came first, the incident or the geographical feature that begs to be brought alive in a story that features some unusual aspect of this location.

There is a giant sandstone boulder about a mile north of Old Laguna, on the road to Paguate. It is ten feet tall and twenty feet in circumference. When I was a child and we would pass this boulder driving to Paguate village, someone usually made reference to the story about Kochininako, Yellow Woman, and the Estrucuyo, a monstrous giant who nearly ate her. The Twin Hero Brothers saved Kochininako, who had been out hunting rabbits to take home to feed her mother and sisters. The Hero Brothers had heard her cries just in time. The Estrucuyo had cornered her in a cave too small to fit its monstrous head. Kochininako had already thrown to the Estrucuyo all her rabbits, as well as her moccasins, and most of her clothing. Still the creature had not been satisfied. After killing the Estrucuyo with her bows and arrows, the Twin Hero Brothers slit open the Estrucuyo and cut out its heart. They threw the heart as far as they could. The monster's heart landed there, beside the old trail to Paguate village, where the sandstone boulder rests now.

It may be argued that the existence of the boulder precipitated the creation of a story to explain it. But sandstone boulders and sandstone formations of strange shapes abound in the Laguna

Pueblo area. Yet, most of them do not have stories. Often the crucial element in a narrative is the terrain—some specific detail of the setting.

A high, dark mesa rises dramatically from a grassy plain, fifteen miles southeast of Laguna, in an area known as Swahnee. On the grassy plain one hundred years ago, my great-grandmother's uncle and his brother-in-law were grazing their herd of sheep. Because visibility on the plain extends for over twenty miles, it wasn't until the two sheepherders came near the high, dark mesa that the Apaches were able to stalk them. Using the mesa to obscure their approach, the raiders swept around from both ends of the mesa. My great-grandmother's relatives were killed, and the herd was lost. The high, dark mesa played a critical role: the mesa had compromised the safety which the openness of the plains had seemed to assure.

Pueblo and Apache alike relied upon the terrain, the very earth itself, to give them protection and aid. Human activities or needs were maneuvered to fit the existing surroundings and conditions. I imagine the last afternoon of my distant ancestors as warm and sunny for late September. They might have been traveling slowly, bringing the sheep closer to Laguna in preparation for the approach of colder weather. The grass was tall and only beginning to change from green to a yellow that matched the late afternoon sun shining off it. There might have been comfort in the warmth and the sight of the sheep fattening on good pasture which lulled my ancestors into their fatal inattention. They might have had a rifle, whereas the Apaches had only bows and arrows. But there would have been four or five Apache raiders, and the surprise attack would have canceled any advantage the rifles gave them.

Survival in any landscape comes down to making the best use of all available resources. On that particular September afternoon, the raiders made better use of the Swahnee terrain than my poor ancestors did. Thus, the high, dark mesa and the story of the two lost Laguna herders became inextricably linked. The memory of them and their story resides in part with the high, dark mesa. For as long as the mesa stands, people within the family and clan will be reminded of the story of that afternoon long ago. Thus, the continuity and accuracy of the oral narratives are reinforced by the landscape—and the Pueblo interpretation of that landscape is *maintained*.

The Migration Story: An Interior Journey

The Laguna Pueblo migration stories refer to specific places— mesas, springs, or cottonwood trees—not only locations that can be visited still, but also locations that lie directly on the state highway route linking Paguate village with Laguna village.[6] In traveling this road as a child with older Laguna people I first heard a few of the stories from that much larger body of stories linked with the Emergence and Migration.[7] It may be coincidental that Laguna people continue to follow the same route that, according to the Migration story, the ancestors followed south from the Emergence Place. It may be that the route is merely the shortest and best route for car, horse, or foot traffic between Laguna and Paguate villages. But if the stories about boulders, springs, and hills are actually remnants from a ritual that retraces the Creation and Emergence of the Laguna Pueblo people as a culture, as the people they became, then con- tinued use of that route creates a unique relationship between the ritual-mythic world and the actual, everyday world. A journey from Paguate to Laguna down the long decline of Paguate Hill retraces the original journey from the Emergence Place, which is located slightly north of the Paguate village. Thus, the landscape between Paguate and Laguna takes on a deeper significance: the landscape resonates the spiritual, or mythic, dimension of the Pueblo world even today.

Although each Pueblo culture designates its Emergence Place, usually a small natural spring edged with mossy sandstone and full of cattails and wild watercress, it is clear the Pueblo people do not view any single location or natural springs as the one and only true Emergence Place. Each Pueblo group recounts stories connected with Creation, Emergence, and Migration, although it is believed that all human beings, with all the animals and plants, emerged at the same place and at the same time.[8]

Natural springs are crucial sources of water for all life in the high desert and plateau country. So the small spring near Paguate village is literally the source and continuance of life for the people in the area. The spring also functions on a spiritual level, recalling the original Emergence Place and linking the people and the spring water to all other people and to that moment when the Pueblo people became aware of themselves as they are even now. The Emergence was an emergence into a precise cultural identity. Thus, the Pueblo stories about the Emergence and Migration are not to be taken as literally as the anthropologists might wish. Prominent geographical features and landmarks that are mentioned in the narratives exist for ritual purposes, not because the Laguna people actually journeyed south for hundreds of years from Chaco Canyon or Mesa Verde, as the archaeologists say, or eight miles from the site of the natural springs at Paguate to the sandstone hilltop at Laguna.[9]

The eight miles, marked with boulders, mesas, springs, and river crossings, are actually a ritual circuit or path that marks the interior journey the Laguna people made: a journey of awareness and imagination in which they emerged from being within the earth and all-included in the earth to the culture and people they became, differentiating themselves for the first time from all that had surrounded them, always aware that interior distances cannot be reckoned in physical miles or in calender years.

The narratives linked with prominent features of the landscape between Paguate and Laguna delineate the complexities of the relationship that human beings must maintain with the surrounding natural world if they hope to survive in this place. Thus, the journey was an interior process of the imagination, a growing awareness that being human is somehow different from all other life—animal, plant, and inanimate. Yet, we are all from the same source: awareness never deteriorated into Cartesian duality, cutting off the human from the natural world.

The people found the opening into the Fifth World too small to allow them or any of the small animals to escape. They had sent a fly out through the small hole to tell them if it was the world the Mother Creator had promised. It was, but there was the problem of getting out. The antelope tried to butt the opening to enlarge it, but the antelope enlarged it only a little. It was necessary for the badger with her long claws to assist the antelope, and at last the opening was enlarged enough so that all the people and animals were able to emerge up into the Fifth World. The human beings could not have emerged without the aid of antelope and badger. The human beings depended upon the aid and charity of the animals. Only through interdependence could the human beings survive. Families belonged to clans, and it was by clan that the human being joined with the animal and plant world. Life on the high, arid plateau became viable when the human beings were able to imagine themselves as sisters and brothers to the badger, antelope, clay, yucca, and sun. Not until they could find a viable relationship to the terrain—the physical landscape they found themselves in—could they *emerge*. Only at the moment that the requisite balance between human and *other* was realized could the Pueblo people become a culture, a distinct group whose population and survival remained stable despite the vicissitudes of the climate and terrain.

Landscape thus has similarities with dreams. Both have the power to seize terrifying feelings and deep instincts and translate them into images—visual, aural, tactile—and into the concrete where human beings may more readily confront and channel the terrifying instincts or powerful emotions into rituals and narratives which reassure the individual while reaffirming cherished values of the group. The identity of the individual as a part of the group and the greater Whole is strengthened, and the terror of facing the world alone is extinguished.

Even now, the people at Laguna Pueblo spend the greater portion of social occasions recounting recent incidents or events that have occurred in the Laguna area. Nearly always, the discussion will precipitate the retelling of older stories about similar incidents or other stories connected with a specific place. The stories often contain disturbing or provocative material, but are nonetheless told in the presence of children and women. The effect of these interfamily or interclan exchanges is the reassurance for each person that she or he will never be separated or apart from the clan, no matter what might happen. Neither the worst blunders or disasters nor the greatest financial prosperity and joy will ever be permitted to isolate anyone from the rest of the group. In the ancient times cohesiveness was all that stood between extinction and survival, and while the individual certainly was recognized, it was always as an individual simultaneously bonded to family and clan by a complex bundle of custom and ritual. You are never the first to suffer a grave loss or profound humiliation. You are never the first, and you understand that you will probably not be the last to commit, or be victimized by, a repugnant act. Your family and clan are able to go on at length about others now passed on and others older or more experienced than you who suffered similar losses.

The wide, deep arroyo near the Kings Bar (located across the reservation's borderline) has over the years claimed many vehicles. A few years ago, a Vietnam veteran's new red Volkswagen rolled backwards into the arroyo while he was inside buying a six-pack of beer; the story of his loss soon joined the lively and large collection of stories already connected with that big arroyo. I do not know whether the Vietnam veteran was consoled when he was told the stories about the other cars claimed by the ravenous arroyo. All of his savings of combat pay had gone to buy the red VW. But this man could not have felt any worse than the man who, some years before, had left his children and mother-in-law in his station-wagon with the engine running. When he came out of the liquor store his station-wagon was gone. He found it and its passengers upside down in the big arroyo: broken bones, cuts, and bruises, and a total wreck of the car.

The big arroyo has a wide mouth. Its existence needs no explanation. People in the area regard the arroyo much as they might regard a living being, which has a certain character and personality. I seldom drive past that wide, deep arroyo without feeling a familiarity and even a strange affection for it, because as treacherous as it may be, the arroyo maintains a strong connection between human beings and the earth. The arroyo demands from us the caution and attention that constitute respect. It is this sort of respect the old believers have in mind when they tell us we must respect and love the earth.

Hopi elders said that the austere and, to some eyes, barren plains and hills surrounding their mesa-top villages (in northeast Arizona) actually help to nurture the spirituality of the Hopi *way*. The Hopi elders say the Hopi people might have settled in locations far more lush, where daily life would not have been so grueling. But there on the high, silent, sandstone mesas that overlook the sandy, arid expanses stretching to all horizons, the Hopi elders say the Hopi people must "live by their prayers" if they are to survive. The Hopi way cherishes the intangible: the riches realized from interaction and interrelationships with all beings above all else. Great abundances of material things, even food, the Hopi elders believe, tend to lure human attention away from what is most valuable and important. The views of the Hopi elders are not much different from those elders in all the Pueblos.

The bare but beautiful vastness of the Hopi landscape emphasizes the visual impact of every plant, every rock, every arroyo. Nothing is overlooked or taken for granted. Each ant, each lizard, each lark is imbued with great value simply because the creature is there, simply because the creature is alive in a place where any life at all is precious. Stand on the mesa's edge at Walpi and look southwest over the bare distances toward the pale blue outlines of the San Francisco Peaks (north of Flagstaff) where the *ka'tsina* spirits reside. So little lies between you and the sky. So little lies between you and the earth. One look and you know that simply to survive is a great triumph, that every possible resource is needed, every possible ally—even the most humble insect or reptile. You realize you will be speaking with all of them if you intend to last out the year. Thus it is that the Hopi elders are grateful to the landscape for aiding them in their quest as spiritual people.

Out under the Sky

My earliest memories are of being outside, under the sky. I remember climbing the fence when I was three years old, and heading for the plaza in the center of Laguna village because other children passing by had told me there were *ka'tsinas* there dancing with pieces of wood in their mouths. A neighbor, a woman, retrieved me before I ever saw the wood-swallowing *ka'tsinas,* but from an early age I knew I wanted to be outside: outside walls and fences.

My father had wandered over all the hills and mesas around Laguna when he was a child, because the Indian school and the taunts of the other children did not sit well with him. It had been difficult in those days to be part Laguna and part white, or *amedicana.* It was still difficult when I attended the Indian school at Laguna. Our full-blooded relatives and clanspeople assured us we were theirs and that we belonged there because we had been born and reared there. But the racism of the wider world we call America had begun to make itself felt years before. My father's response was to head for the mesas and hills with his older brother, their dog, and .22 rifles. They retreated to the sandstone cliffs and juniper forests. Out in the hills they were not lonely because they had all the living creatures of the hills around them, and, whatever the ambiguities of racial heritage, my father and uncle understood what the old folks had taught them: the earth loves all of us regardless, because we are her children.

I started roaming those same mesas and hills when I was nine years old. At eleven I rode away on my horse and explored places my father and uncle could not have reached on foot. I was never afraid or lonely—though I was high in the hills, many miles from home—because I carried with me the feeling I'd acquired from listening to the old stories, that the land all around me was teeming with creatures that were related to human beings and to me. The stories had also left me with a feeling of familiarity and warmth for the mesas, hills, and boulders where the incidents or action in the stories had taken place. I felt as if I had actually been to those places, although I had only heard stories about them. Somehow the stories had given a kind of being to the mesas and hills, just as the stories had left me with the sense of having spent time with the people in the stories, though they had long since passed on.

It is remarkable to sense the presence of those long passed at the locations where their adventures took place. Spirits range without boundaries of any sort, and spirits may be called back in any number of ways. The method used in the calling also determines how the spirit manifests itself. I think a spirit may or may not choose to remain at the site of its passing or death. I think they might be in a number of places at the same time. Storytelling can procure fleeting moments to experience who they were and how life felt long ago. What I enjoyed most as a child was standing at the site of an incident recounted in one of the ancient stories that Old Aunt Susie had told us as girls. What excited me was listening to her tell us an old-time story and then realizing that I was familiar with a certain mesa or cave that figured as the central location of the story she was telling. That was when the stories worked best, because then I could sit there listening and be able to visualize myself as being located *within* the story being told, within the landscape. Because the storytellers did not just tell the stories, they would in their way act them out. The storyteller would imitate voices for vast dialogues between the various figures in the story. So we sometimes say the moment is alive again within us, within our imaginations and our memory, as we listen.

Aunt Susie once told me how it had been when she was a child and her grandmother agreed to tell the children stories. The old woman would always ask the youngest child in the room to go open the door. "Go open the door," her grandmother would say. "Go open the door so our esteemed ancestors may bring us the precious gift of their stories." Two points seem clear: the spirits could be present, and the stories were valuable because they taught us how we were the people we believed we were. The myth, the web of memories and ideas that create an identity, is a part of oneself. This sense of identity was intimately linked with the surrounding terrain, to the landscape that has often played a significant role in a story or in the outcome of a conflict.

The landscape sits in the center of Pueblo belief and identity. Any narratives about the Pueblo people necessarily give a great deal of attention and detail to all aspects of a landscape. For this reason, the Pueblo people have always been extremely reluctant to relinquish their land for dams or highways. For this reason, Taos Pueblo fought from 1906 to 1973 to win back its sacred Blue Lake, which was illegally taken by the creation of Taos National Forest. For this reason, the decision in the early 1950s to begin open-pit mining of the huge uranium deposits north of Laguna, near Paguate village, has had a powerful psychological impact upon the Laguna people. Already a large body of stories has grown up around the subject of what happens to people who disturb or destroy the earth. I was a child when the mining began and the apocalyptic warning stories were being told. And I have lived long enough to begin hearing the stories that verify the early warnings.

All that remains of the gardens and orchards that used to grow in the sandy flats southeast of Paguate village are the stories of the lovely big peaches and apricots the people used to grow. The Jackpile Mine is an open pit that has been blasted out of the many hundreds of acres where the orchards and melon patches once grew. The Laguna people have not witnessed changes to the land without strong reactions. Descriptions of the landscape *before* the mine are as vivid as any description of the present-day destruction by the open-pit mining. By its very ugliness and by the violence it does to the land, the Jackpile Mine insures that, from now on, it, too, will be included in the vast body of narratives that makes up the history of the Laguna people and the Pueblo landscape. And the description of what that landscape looked like *before* the uranium mining began will always carry considerable impact.

Landscape as a Character in Fiction

When I began writing I found that the plots of my short stories very often featured the presence of elements out of the landscape, elements that directly influenced the outcome of events. Nowhere is landscape more crucial to the outcome than in my short story, "Storyteller." The site is southwest Alaska in the Yukon Delta National Wildlife Refuge, near the village of Bethel, on the Kuskokwim River. Tundra country. Here the winter landscape can suddenly metamorphose into a seamless, blank white so solid that pilots in aircraft without electronic instruments lose their bearings and crash their planes into the frozen tundra, believing down to be up. Here on the Alaskan tundra, in mid-February, not all the space-age fabrics, electronics, or engines can ransom human beings from the restless, shifting forces of the winter sky and winter earth.

The young Yupik Eskimo woman works out an elaborate yet subconscious plan to avenge the deaths of her parents. After months of baiting the trap, she lures the murderer onto the river's ice where he falls through to his death. The murderer is a white man who operated the village trading post. For years the murderer has existed like a parasite, exploiting not only the fur-bearing animals and the fish, but also the Yupik people themselves. When the Yupik woman kills him, the white trader has just finished cashing in on the influx of workers who have suddenly come to the tiny village for the petroleum exploration and pipeline.

For the Yupik people, souls deserving punishment spend varying lengths of time in a place of freezing. The Yupik see the world's end coming with ice, not fire. Although the white trader possessed every possible garment, insulation, heating fuel, and gadget ever devised to protect him from the frozen tundra environment, he still dies, drowning under the freezing river ice, because the white man had not reckoned with the true power of that landscape, especially not the power that the Yupik woman understood instinctively and which she used so swiftly and efficiently. The white man had reckoned with the young woman and determined he could overpower her. But the white man had failed to account for the conjunction of the landscape with the woman. The Yupik woman had never seen herself as anything but a part of that sky, that frozen river, that tundra. The river's ice and the blinding white are her accomplices, and yet the Yupik woman never for a moment misunderstands her own relationship with that landscape.

After the white trader has crashed through the river's ice, the young woman finds herself a great distance from either shore of the treacherous, frozen river. She can see nothing but the whiteness of the sky swallowing the earth. But far away in the distance, on the side of her log and tundra-sod cabin, she is able to see a spot of bright red: a bright red marker she had nailed up weeks earlier because she was intrigued by the contrast between all that white and the spot of brilliant red. The Yupik woman knows the appetite of the frozen river. She realizes that the ice and the fog, the tundra and the snow seek constantly to be re-united with the living beings which skitter across it. The Yupik woman knows that inevitably she and all things will one day lie in those depths. But the woman is young and her instinct is to live. The Yupik woman knows how to do this.

Inside the small cabin of logs and tundra sod, the old storyteller is mumbling the last story he will ever tell. It is the story of the hunter stalking a giant polar bear the color of the blue glacier ice. It is a story that the old storyteller has been telling since the young Yupik woman began to arrange the white trader's death:

> *A sudden storm develops. The hunter finds himself on an ice floe offshore. Visibility is zero, and the scream of the wind blots out all sound. Quickly the hunter realizes he is being stalked, hunted by all the forces, by all the elements of the sky and earth around him. When at last the hunter's own muscles spasm and cause the jade knife to fall and shatter the ice, the hunter's death in the embrace of the giant, ice blue bear is the foretelling of the world's end.*

When humans have blasted and burned the last bit of life from the earth, an immeasurable freezing will descend with a darkness that obliterates the sun.

BREAKING THE SILENCE

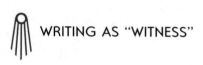 WRITING AS "WITNESS"

Gloria Bird

On November 29, 1990, President George Bush signed into law PL 101-644, the Indian Arts and Crafts Act of 1990, which requires Native artists to prove their Native heritage. The impetus behind this law seems to have been to protect the investors in Indian art rather than the interests of Native people. One consequence of the law was to drive a wedge between Native artists, who are now divided over the issue of Native identity. Among Native artists, blacklists of artists of questionable descent appeared, and recently Native writers have been called into question in a three-part exposé in the *Lakota Times* section of *Indian Country Today*.[1] Ultimately, the go-for-the-jugular psychology of government agencies intent on colonizing the minds of the people rests on the policy of dividing and conquering, keeping us bickering among ourselves in order to distract us from the larger issues that affect our lives. For example, recent legislation introduced in Congress is a repetition of the termination policies of the 1950s and of the strategy of targeting nontreaty tribes. Likewise, the ongoing negotiation for tribal lands to become garbage dumps for the nation's nuclear waste is a reality.

Coming at a time when countless pending issues face Native peoples—and when our loyalties are divided as well on the home front—it behooves us to move toward a common ground as Native people, to take back that power over us that is constantly imposed on us from the outside. I acknowledge that Native people lobbied for a law governing Indian art, which demonstrates the degree to which we have internalized the mainstream consciousness of what "Indian" is: a commodity with marketable value. Ascribing false power to the distinctions we are making serves only to separate us, while our less functional parts can be manipulated to the point that we eye one another with suspicion. Somehow the tenacious spirit of our ancestors, which has guided us to this point, has gone astray.

In a recent lengthy discussion, the Lakota author and scholar Elizabeth Cook-Lynn mentioned that the personal story in her Native community is not "the story that we tell." She did not see the value of her personal autobiography as an addition to Native literature, her interpretation of that category being modeled after Native storytelling, which is communal and which serves a multiplicity of purposes too complex to go into here. The seeming incompatibility between one's personal story and Native narrative forms needs to be resolved before this essay can continue.

Two things occur to me. First, as a Native writer must I always position the act of creativity with respect to a Native, and if so, does that not limit the scope of my writing? I would like to believe it does not. This question leads to the second question: What is Native literature? The answer to the second question, prompted by the challenge raised by one of my colleagues in the field of Native literature, is one that I hope Native writers and Native academics will someday reach a consensus upon. (And here I must interject that, yes, I am saying that specifically *Native* writers and *Native* academics need to take control of the dialogue, to define their literary traditions in the same manner that other nationalist literary movements have done.) To me as a writer, everything is motivated by a political agenda. Indeed, being Indian in the United States is inherently political, and as both Joy Harjo and Audre

Lorde have written, "We were never meant to survive."[2] In light of this, I see my personal story as bearing witness to colonization and my writing as a testimony aimed at undoing those processes that attempt to keep us in the grips of the colonizer's mental bondage.

Because we are aware of the marginalization of Indian communities in the media and of the necessity for corporations, government agencies, and military and police networks to cloak their activities on Indian lands, the idea of "witnessing" provides political leverage. The political employment of witnessing occurred during the occupation of Wounded Knee in 1973, and because that old stand-by the divide-and-conquer routine appeared again, witnessing was again employed by the Portland Big Mountain Support Group, who flocked to the Four Corners area in support of the dispossessed Diné from newly designated Hopi land in 1988. (I must intrude again to point out that while my interpretation of these complex events may seem simplistic, I mention them only as examples.) What is understood is that our position within a system that is designed to deny us is tenuous and continually threatened and that there is truly strength in the numbers of witnesses who can carry our stories outward. Not long ago, as I conducted research on the Nez Perce Retreat of 1877 (otherwise known as a "war"), I searched for the written testimonies of women and children on the events and occupations of the people during that historical period. Thus both witnessing and testimony become, for me, viable tools that serve the purposes of decolonization by providing details of individual processing of the complexities of inheritance that living in the aftermath of colonization provides.

Autobiography is important to undoing the process of the colonization of our minds. I see the process of colonization as multilayered. Physical colonization includes the loss of lands, lives, and livelihood. Enough has been written about the underlying motives for those conditions. The hardest work is tracing back through generations the aspects of colonization that have directly affected our lives, to identify those instances in which we have internalized what we are taught about ourselves in schools and in history books all of our invisible lives: that we have no history of our own, at least none that has been recognized. If we consider, for instance, the circumstances of our immediate family; our tribal history; the dynamics of our individual groups; the "old ways," including the belief systems and values; and lastly the part that education and organized religion have played, we gain an insight into our individual development in the ongoing process of colonization. The benefits to be gained from this type of work include the weakening of the burden of inherited shame, loss, dispossession, and disconnectedness. Yet writing remains more than a catharsis; at its liberating best, it is a political act. Through writing we can undo the damaging stereotypes that are continually perpetuated about Native peoples. We can rewrite our history, and we can mobilize our future.

My story shares similarities with the experiences of other Native people who were reared on reservations. A complex of strains on our communities exists as a result of colonization—the conversion to Christianity, for example. While I focus here on some of the issues conversion to Christianity raises for me personally, I feel a need to ask that the reader focus less on the perceived pain that has been handed down through the generations and more on the larger issue of decolonization of the mind that comes with identifying the source of the pain in order to be free of its power over us.

In the Northwest, the relationship of the people to the land is dictated by the seasons and the availability of Indian foods. We are hunter-gatherer people. One of the last times I was home, I found my mother outside her home in Nespelem, tending fires while she cooked camas in the old-time way. I entered the house and was immediately engulfed by the pungent and distinctive smell of baked camas and was thrown back into the olfactory impressions of my childhood: entering the old people's homes surrounded by the comforting smell of smoked hide and Indian foods. When my mother entered the house, her face was flushed. She proudly removed the camas from the oven, uncovering the glass baking dish that held her first batch—large brown bulbs with a sticky coating. These, and others that were baking in the pit, were being prepared for the Longhouse meals.

The food, the land, and the ritual of root gathering and berry picking, with the ensuing feasts, are all part of both history and the present, and as I discovered, these events, which dictated my mother's daily and seasonal occupations, were also dictating mine in a very different way. Until that day I had only *read* of baking camas, though their familiar smell was a part of my early life. Because these roots were being prepared for the Root Feast, the first of the traditional dinners held in the Longhouse, I had not tasted any of my mother's camas.

My relationship to my homeland, and that of the people of the Northwest in general, involves identifying not so much with a single reservation as with a larger territory. I was born in the Yakama Valley[3] in a hospital that is no longer there and grew up on both the Colville Reservation and the Spokane Reservation, of which I am a tribal member. All of our peoples were seasonally on the move and were familiar with food trails that are still there in the memories of the older people. As we often drove northwest from the city of Spokane to Nespelem, a distance of just over a hundred miles, I recall hearing stories of how the people traveled by buckboard to gather roots on these same plains, now covered over by miles of wheat. There are still small patches of bitterroot to be found right off the highway on private property.

Most of my early years were spent outdoors with plenty of time to explore the habitat with my sisters. It was my older sister who taught me how to peel sunflower stalks and eat them with a little salt. Scavenging the outdoors, we learned to eat pine nuts from pine cones (a tedious business which didn't hold our interest for long), to chew pine needles from the trees, and to dig potato flowers for their bulbous roots. My mother chewed "tree gum," which stuck to our teeth and for which we never developed a taste; we found berries more to our liking. When we were lucky, we found thornberry bushes and ate thornberries by the handful, seeds and all. We ate the gooseberries that grew untended next to our grandparents' water pump. And we found patches of wild strawberries—smaller than the domesticated kinds but darker and sweeter.

Oregon grapes grow on a shrub that is low to the ground. They're a bitter-tasting, small, purple berry that my grandmother made into jelly for my grandfather. He was the only person I know of—besides myself—who liked to eat Oregon grapes. My grandfather also had a taste for *skoosum,* made from "foam berries" and called "Indian ice cream" in English. My grandmother canned the juice in Gerber Baby Food jars. I also loved the tartness of skoosum and was amazed that such a small amount could be whipped into stiff, thick peaks that filled a bread bowl.

During the summers I lived in my grandparents' house in Chewelah, Washington, where the past and the present merged. In our Salishan language, *chewelah* means "water snake," and the valley was given its name after the many water snakes that once inhabited the small river running through the valley floor. The Chewelah band who lived in the valley are buried in a small, old graveyard that is barely visible from the highway that cuts north and south through the town. These people are called *slawtews,* and my grand-mother is the oldest living descendant of these people and the only Indian who still owns property in the valley. The Chewelah Valley was their traditional wintering place, and it was from there that they began traveling to the fishing sites and the berry picking and root digging places.

The Spokane Reservation, located in eastern Washington forty-five miles northwest of the city of Spokane, was created by executive order in 1881. The Chewelah band, a Kalispel band of the Flathead, were given the choice of joining either the Spokane or Colville Reservations, and they chose to join the Spokane, who were closer to their original home. During the allotment period, the Chewelah band members were given 160-acre allotments. Soon afterward, with the exception of two allotments—She-She-Tay's and that belonging to the last Chewelah chief—these lands were sold. When my great-grandmother inherited the property, she refused to sell. When she became elderly and bedridden, she was persuaded by my grandmother's brother, who was then the Spokane tribal chairman, that selling the property was for the best. How he convinced her to put her fingerprint on the paperwork is unknown.

From that sale my grandmother was given enough to pur-chase a new homesite; her sister was disinherited by her brothers; one brother received enough to pay off his many debts; and the oldest brother, who had connived to sell out, received the most cash profit from the sale. My grandmother later sold the property to the wheat farmer whose fields surrounded the old homesite on the condition that my grandparents would not move until after my great-grandmother's death. As my mother says, "That is how we became homeless." With the knowledge that the land had been lost, my great-grandmother simply faded away.

The complex of small wood-frame houses and sheds that made up my grandparents' home was surrounded by wheat fields. In the center was the tar-papered house that my mother remembers living in with my great-grandmother. Though we called it Yi ya's house, in my memories my great-grandmother had already moved into the main house, where she was bedridden with a broken hip, and her house was being used for storage. *Yi ya* is the term for grandmother which, as children, we addressed our great-grandmother by, although the accurate term would have been *tu pi ya*. Also, the old aunts who came to visit were *tu pi yas*. Yi ya spoke only a handful of English words. My younger sister and I slept in the same room with her. When we would call out to her each night, "Good night, Yi ya," she would always answer, "Good night, Yi ya." As children, we were never sure why she addressed us in this way, but I suspect that in the old ways children were recognized as being inheritors of the longer memories. After my great-grandmother passed away, my grandparents moved. The main house was also moved in pieces—that is, whole rooms—that were reassembled to become a shed and garage adjacent to the new house, still in Chewelah. The old homesite is now covered by wheat.

In my memory of my grandfather, he was always a great teaser who liked to sit at the table with us while we ate. He would become serious and ask, "How come every time your elbow bends, your mouth opens? See, like that." Or he would pull us onto his lap and say, "You have a hole under your arm, look here," which was his excuse to tickle us. He was also a great storyteller, not of the old legends but of entertaining kinds of stories. He was very animated, using his hands to talk and modulating his voice to fit his stories. My grandfather had five brothers, and in old family photos many of the brothers are together. I recall a time when my grandfather and his brothers were on the porch at the new homesite in Chewelah, playing their fiddles and dancing together. The older people were a social people; they came together to visit, to share stories and meals, and to dance.

Not only was my grandfather a great storyteller, he was also one of the few people who still spoke the older language and used words of which people no longer remembered the meanings. In my grandparents' house, the relatives often spent long hours arguing over the meaning of words in our language. Fascinated, I would eavesdrop on these discussions. It was through this eavesdropping that I learned that my mother also knew the older words and their meanings. I grew up in a household where Indian was spoken all around me but never to me. I would sit on the periphery, unable to comprehend, though I did manage to learn a few words. This experience precipitated my love of language.

In my grandparents' house I learned that, though it contradicted "Indian" lifeways, Christianity still played a part in our lives. The Jesuits converted the Spokane Tribe, and most of the people were Catholic, including Yi ya and my grandmother. My mother told me a story that her grandmother had told her about the priests' practice of extorting confessions from people. Yi ya told my mother about her first confession when she was a young girl. The priest asked my great-grandmother a series of questions, including, "Do you do dirty, nasty things with boys?" Yi ya told my mother that she had nodded and answered yes to all of the questions put to her by the priest in this fashion, although none of his charges had been true. My mother asked her why she answered yes if she did not do such things, to which her grandmother explained that it was easier this way. The priest would dole out some penance and go on his way.

When my mother told me this, she spoke with pride of her grandmother, who though she practiced Catholicism did so with tongue in cheek. She had not given up on her Indian ways altogether. In Yi ya's mind, what a priest thought or what his motives were for extorting fabricated confessions made little difference.

My great-grandmother's attitude was very different from the kind of Catholicism practiced by my grandmother. The strains of our family heritage are divided: Some of the family remain "Indian," and some have ties that are closer to the Catholic religion. Two of my aunts, influenced by their mother's showing disgust at "Indians" and totally embracing the Catholic religion, married white men and reared their families at a great distance from the reservation. Of those children, I know of at least one whom I consider to be mad with fanaticism and who works only to support her many journeys to visit shrines in the Holy Land. How bizarre to have a first cousin by blood who does not know that the holiest land is the place where the bones of our ancestors, the *slawtews,* lie in the little graveyard in the Chewelah Valley. I also have first cousins who are blond and blue-eyed, revealing the fact that several generations back on my grandmother's side there was a white man. Though that detail was common knowledge among our family members, it was not important enough to talk about or to be concerned about enough to hide. Blood quantum had not yet become an issue.

What was unmentioned but not unacknowledged was the fact that my mother, the eldest, was not the biological daughter of the man I knew as my grandfather. No one seems to know the details of how this happened. My blood grandfather was a man I never knew, though I know that he was Flathead.

In my family history, then, there is this tension between the old ways, being Indian, the speaking of our Native language, Catholicism, and family silences. The things that were never spoken of impacted directly upon my childhood through the way that we, as the offspring of my mother, were perceived by those caregivers among the larger community, including our extended family, but I learned of them only later as I became an adult with my own children. Imagine the sense of betrayal I felt to find that the man whom I loved as my grandfather was not a blood relative at all. Still, in the Indian way, he remains my grandfather.

This knowledge explains for me the antagonism between my grandmother and my mother which often erupted into arguments that I never understood as a child. It explains the hostility that my mother's sisters, my aunts, felt toward her throughout their adulthood. It also explains why my mother was so much darker than the rest of our family. I have inherited, along with all of the good memories of childhood, the undertow of pain and disappointment, and in my life I have felt the poignancy of silences which, because of this writing, I am now breaking.

At the death of my great-grandmother, Louise She-She-Tay, no one came to rescue me from the mission boarding school to attend her wake or funeral. Instead, my grandmother wrote a letter to tell me of her passing. In her scrawling hand she advised me, "Pray to the Blessed Virgin, she can help you." I felt a deep anger settle in, the roots of which went back generations. As a child, I could not acknowledge the feelings of anger and resentment, which were in opposition to the respect for our elders that we were taught as Indian children. At times our very culture immobilizes us. I felt that my right to grieve was being denied; I had loved my Yi ya deeply. I resented being handed an empty-faced Catholic idol to replace the loving, kind face of my great-grandmother, who spoke Salish and who called me Girl. In more ways than one, I resented how the religion that she so desperately clung to had stolen my grandmother from me.

It had also robbed my mother of her mother because if my grandmother had not learned to feel shame, she would not have rejected her daughter. My mother was raised with the stigma of having shamed my grandmother. I don't know whether there ever was any love between them, but I knew and felt love from my grandfather and from my great-grandmother. I can understand the dynamics of the relationships between the other relatives, though it is difficult for me even as an adult to forgive my grandmother for turning her children against one another and for inevitably turning our family inside out. We are all still trapped within that paradigm, inheritors of division, each of us struggling in our own way toward resolution and healing.

My grandmother lives in the convalescent center in Chewe-lah. I have not visited her or spoken to her since my grandfather's funeral some eighteen years ago. His passing left a vacant place in my feelings for the valley and the house they lived in. At his wake I was jolted to realize I had no personal relationship with my grand-mother to speak of; we had nothing left to talk about. Once, when we found ourselves alone in the house and as she sat beading in her rocker, I could feel her discomfort and heard the strained edge in her voice as she commented on the weather or the soap opera that was playing on the TV. I don't recall answering her, but I do re-member the silence that was passed down from mother to daughter and again from mother to daughter. I also do not forget the nurtur-ing care given to me by my grandmother over the years in which we spent our summers in her house. Perhaps it is a blessing that in her old age she is afflicted with senility; so much of her life would be too painful to remember.

My mother, on the other hand, is still resiliently alive, and the older she gets, the more she tells me about growing up with Yi ya and about the Indian beliefs and ways that she practices in her life. She is a root digger, one of the group of women who seasonally go out to gather the roots needed for traditional dinners. She drums and sings with a small drum group. She is the one who makes the dancing outfits for the children of our family—their moccasins, shawls, and ribbon shirts. She has named every one of her children, grandchildren, and great-grandchildren with the names of our ancestors. It is my mother who keeps our family together. She is also the one who keeps the family lineage.

My mother once gave me the names of our ancestors for the five generations preceding mine, and in that family tree my grandfather's great-grandmother's name is given as Lays-on-the-Ground. Except for the She-She-Tays from my grandmother's side of the family, everyone has English first and last names. Not long ago, she gave me a yellowed copy of the "Do You Remember?" page of the tribal newspaper that contained a photograph of her father. I now have a face to attach to his name. My mother is the link to our past, and without her knowledge I would not be able to pass this on to my children.

There is the personal sense of loss that, placed in perspective, can be overcome and understood in ways that do not necessarily have to be damaging. There is also the reality of exploitation of the land that colonized people must face. Indian nations bear the brunt of the government-sanctioned sale (read, theft) of tribal lands, water, and minerals at bargain-basement prices.[4] It is no different for the Spokane Tribe, which either knowingly or inadvertently participates in the exploitation of their—our—lands. Just the other day, the *Wenatchee World* ran an article entitled, "Uranium Mine on Reservation Is Leaking."[5] The reportage is, however, belated.

On the Spokane Reservation there are two open-pit uranium mines, the Sherwood Mine (operated by Western Nuclear, a subsidiary of Phelps Dodge) and the Midnight Mine (operated by the Dawn Mining Company of the Newmont Corporation). I would like to include a little history from "An Investigation into Mining Pollution on the Spokane Indian Reservation, Washington," a personal, unpublished document compiled by Dolores Castillo, my sister, in February 1985:

> The first commercial uranium deposit in the Pacific Northwest was found on the Spokane Indian Reservation. Although a number of other uranium occurrences were found in eastern Washington and Idaho, Montana and Oregon, none were as large or as important as the Midnight Mine deposit. To date this property has produced most of the uranium mined in the four northwest states.
>
> A mining lease agreement between Dawn Mining Company and the Spokane Tribe of Indians was made in September, 1955. . . . Detailed mill design work started in mid-August of 1956 and construction began later that year. . . . Production of uranium ore began in the spring of 1957 and milling operations began in August, 1957. During that year, 592,000 tons of waste were stripped, 164,000 tons of ore were mined, and 151,000 tons of low-grade material, "protore," were stockpiled. . . .
>
> Mining is by open-pit bench methods. Because of

this method, overburden and waste material are stock-piled within the mine boundaries. In addition, low-grade protore is stockpiled for possible future milling.

The house we once lived in sat just off the main road running through the heart of the reservation, and uranium trucks regularly drove by in thick clouds of dust. At the farthest corner of the property, a uranium truck loaded with ore ran off the road and ended up on its side in our field. Later the truck was removed, but some of the stone was left behind. Inspecting the scene, I picked up a piece of uranium ore, fascinated with its coloring: gray stone with streaks of turquoise that reminded me of oxidized copper. I brought the rock to school, where our teacher placed it on the windowsill and where it was handled by each of my classmates. Then, no one knew the danger to humans living near open-pit uranium mines and tailings ponds—or at least the ones who knew certainly weren't about to tell us.

Years later, in 1976, I began working in an environmental library in Santa Fe, New Mexico. I read environmental impact statements and government publications on the health hazards to people living near open-pit mines and mill-tailings ponds. I en-rolled in Evergreen State College's Independent Studies Program that fall to continue doing research on the subject. I learned that within a hundred-mile radius of open-pit mines there are epi-demics of three types of cancer, that certain types of radioactivity concentrate in the reproductive organs, and that the smaller the body mass, the higher the concentration. The danger posed comes from breathing in radioactive particles released from the mines, which begins an inevitable process of decay.

In the late 1970s, the tribe had buried an unspecified radioac-tive deposit in the smaller community of Ford—the site of the first mill-tailings pond in which the tailings had been stored above-ground. This site is adjacent to one of the main waterways of the reservation. The tribal newspaper had run an article which stated that the storage containers were "guaranteed for fifteen years." I wrote a letter to the *Rawhide Press,* the recently revived tribal news-paper, listing the bleak outlook for our future if the land was not reclaimed. Not long afterward, I lost all tribal funding to continue my studies.

While my research was concerned with the dangers posed to humans living near mill-tailings ponds, my sister's report was specifically concerned with mining pollution. In addition to the open-pit mines, there are two on-site mill-tailings ponds, as I men-tioned above, an aboveground storage deposit of tailings, and stor-age containers of unspecified materials. All of these endanger the lives of the people living in the area.

Yet another source of contamination and environmental damage is the accumulation of water from increased runoff in what is referred to as Pit Number 3 at the Sherwood Mine. In a recent letter from my sister, she told me that during one year there was more runoff than usual and that Pit Number 3 had filled to the brim with water, forming a beautiful but deadly crystalline lake that threatened to overflow. The pit is located about seven miles from the main community of Wellpinit. In addition, the mine is drained by three intermittent streams whose water eventually flows into Lake Roosevelt. To prevent the pit from overflowing, an earthen dam was built to hold back the 250-foot-deep lake of contaminated waste.

Reclamation of the mine sites and the waste dump has been a concern of both the tribe and federal officials. Water quality moni-toring was established in 1979 to "determine if water from the mine dumps had spread beyond the mine site," which included testing of both surface and ground waters. The result of submitting the report directly to the BIA–Portland Area Office by the Water Resources Division of the U.S. Geological Survey in 1983 was to declare the mine drainage site a Hazardous Waste Site.[6] Although directly impacting the Spokane, this information is not common knowledge among its members. The general public has been even less informed of the dangerous environmental threat the mines and waste dumps on the reservation pose to the health of humans.

When the second mine was in full operation, I heard various rumors from people who worked at the mines: that the yellow cake (refined uranium ore that has a powdery yellow appearance) was of the highest quality but that the tribe was being underpaid by the company; that the raw uranium was being exported out of the country; and that we now had a "dead" stream on the reservation, a stream that empties into the Spokane River. Each of these claims is supported by my sister's report. In the aftermath of the mining activity, the number of people dying of cancer continues to rise.

As a mirror of what is being done to the land on the Spokane Reservation—one of the most beautiful areas of the country, with an abundance of natural springs, lakes, forests, animal life, and vegetation—the spirit of the people is festering. There is a subdued depression that manifests itself in high suicide rates, alcoholism, drug- and alcohol-related violence, and death, the effects of which are compounded by higher rates of cancer and economic instability. It is not the kind of place I would raise my children. In my heart, I carry many good memories of growing up in that place, but there are very real concerns that have led me to the decision never to return to the reservation.

I spent the second part of my childhood growing up on the Colville Reservation, which is bounded on the east and south by the

Columbia River adjoining the Spokane Reservation, where my mother now lives and where I return to as my second home. The land there feels old; even the hills are worn as smooth as river stones. Both my mom and dad are active in the Nez Perce community, the members of whom are the direct descendants of Chief Joseph's Wallowa band.[7] One of my sisters now lives there, as do my eldest daughter and grandchildren.

My ties to the land there, to the people and their history, inspired one of my longest ongoing writing projects, "Scattered Red Roots: Poetry on the Nez Perce Retreat of 1877." I began reading historical accounts of the Nez Perce's attempt to reach Canada and of the life of Chief Joseph. What was missing from the various accounts was the obvious lack of a portrayal of Chief Joseph as a humane man, or of writings that testified to his character, which caused him to be designated as a spokesperson for his people. My research became more focused as I looked for any inkling of Joseph as a human being. Key to my understanding of the events was the Nez Perce's familiarity with the land. They were not running helter-skelter across the country but were following food trails that they traveled seasonally. Their territory included parts of Oregon, Washington, Idaho, and western Montana, and each of their campsites was connected to the availability of food in the area. I had just written a poem entitled "The Roots" in which I included the "recipe" for baking camas—taken from a reading source—when on returning home for a visit I found my mother baking her camas in a fire pit in their backyard.

Not long ago, when asked to clarify for a group of students whether I wrote as a Native or as a woman, I was hard-pressed to answer. The question puzzled me then, and it still does, because I realize that as a writer, a Native, and a woman, whatever I write is inevitably informed by experiences that in turn are informed by the processes of socialization and colonization. It is curious that I would be asked to isolate from all of these a single aspect of what makes up my being—that I am a Native or a woman—and to simplify into bare terms what that *means,* glossing over process to discuss product.

For me, writing is a continuing process and involves the processing of information received from life experience. What seems relevant are the areas in which colonization and socialization intersect. I was not reared in what I will call a "traditional" home, for lack of a better term. I believe that the major issues of my life center around my grandmother's Catholicism and how that has shaped our family dynamics. It is one thing to be critical of her and another to acknowledge that she, too, was a product of colonization.

During my grandmother's and my mother's lifetimes, the people were taught to be ashamed of being Indian. More so than her siblings, my mother looked Indian: she was dark-skinned with high cheekbones. It wasn't until later in life that she came to value the things that she learned in the early years spent with her grandmother, the things that she now shares every chance she gets. What she has learned over the course of her life—her mistakes and regrets concerning child rearing, among other things—are what we talk about during my infrequent visits home. These have given me an admiration for my mother, whom I don't see as being locked into stasis about her life, and I attempt to interrogate her own early, accepted ideas against newfound knowledge. There should be a balance between empirical knowledge and learned knowledge. For my mother, the importance of her early life with her grandmother has coalesced with her life now as part of a "traditional" Indian community.

I'm positive that if my grandmother had been more loving toward my mother, that relationship would have actually *aided* in the demise of our family as Native people, as "Indians." So, while I regret that my mother experienced unnecessary pain, she was also given great gifts by her grandmother, who taught her survival skills. There was something of value to make up for emotional neglect. I shudder to think how things might have been different if my mother had been influenced by my grandmother's Catholicism. Would I be lost, blindly running toward the Holy Land today?

My people were missionized in the early 1800s, and my grandmother's generation was the first to be taken away to mission schools. They were taught to sew and set tables, and they were kept from their people for years. They were forbidden to speak their own language, though my mother has told me they did anyway among themselves. This was the generation of the old ladies whom I remember visiting at my grandparents' house, the tu pi yas who would sit and talk in Indian. They shared food and spoke of picking huckleberries in the mountains. The information became a lifeline for those ladies, who were caught between the old ways and the ways they had learned from their experience of being "educated" and Christianized. I think it must have been more difficult for them and their children than it was for my great-grandmother's generation, or for my own.

As Native people, most of us grapple with complex social issues. The most important thing we can do is to move toward a resolution in walking through the most painful moments of our histories to liberation. In talking about my experiences with other Native people, and in comparing our life stories, the parallels in our experience become clear, though we come from varying backgrounds and cultures. Some of us create art, some of us write, and some of us talk. In doing so, we foment the testimony of Native people as witnesses, manifesting our perceptions of the world in useful, creative ways. As a writer, I am unable to discuss how I know myself as "Indian" or where I come from or what the influences have been on my writing without discussing the many interconnected and convoluted issues that have intersected in my life.

The details of my story are given here not as a point of interest in and of themselves but as a vehicle to deconstruct the images of Indians as victims in this war dance in the blood of colonization. Through the generations, those processes that have formed my family and my inheritance from them have impressed upon me many things: the conflicting feelings of a love of homeland and a sense of despair at the destruction of that homeland, and a comfort in hearing the sounds of our Salish language being spoken along with the exclusion I have experienced in not speaking or understanding that language, though that feeling of exclusion was tempered by an appreciation *for* language.

My writing reveals the strained relations between the factions of my family—the Catholics and the "Indians"—and a resultant wrestling with past and present conditions. But through this writing there comes, also, a recognition of my own vulnerability. As a witness, my testimony can only presume to speak from one perspective, my own, which is now open for critical examination and potential attack from both within and without the Native community. Academics argue against what they perceive as essentialism, my basic tendency. And because I do not reside on the reservation, my representation of that community can certainly be questioned. But possibly more to the point is the fact that my definition of self may be wrongly perceived as impeding another's self-definition. I am motivated, however, by the belief that it is only through a critique of where I come from that the act of witnessing and the testimony I offer can become a decolonizing strategy.

Colonization is a relationship, after all. By looking critically at how we have been constructed as "Indian," and by interrogating the ways in which we become complicit in the perpetuation of both the stereotyping and the romanticizing of Indian people, can we take the first step toward undoing the damage that colonization has wrought. If we are not attentive, we can easily be swayed into accepting notions of ourselves as vanishing or somehow inferior, doomed, and tragic, as well as falling prey to the romanticism of "Indians" who have been appropriated to serve other needs. For instance, the Noble Savage of pop culture and American literature; "Indians" as the first environmentalists (the Green Indian syndrome); or "Indians" as mystics (the white shamanist movement). But I trust that as some of us watch the film version of *The Last of the Mohicans* we will come to recognize that *that is not me*. And if I view that representation of Native people as a distortion, my alternative is to offer another version of self to counter that one.

I've come to the conclusion that the politics and social concerns that surround Native representation and existence are of primary importance to me as a writer and need to be addressed. In the end, then, I agree with my writer friend who said she didn't feel her story was important to Native literature. In and of itself, my story is not important either. What makes it important are the other relevant issues that surround us as Native people and that are the context in which I am presenting my story. Without that discussion, telling my story would simply be parading my ethnicity. I need to believe that my story serves a useful purpose. I also mean to make it clear that my primary audience is Native people. We have so much work to do. As a powerful woman once wrote, "If we do not define ourselves, we will be defined by others for their use and to our detriment."[8] I agree, and so I write.

 IN THE CYCLE OF THE WHIRL

Esther G. Belin

Re-Entry

My mother is my story.

She sacrificed for me, allowing me to use the enemy's tongue. Perhaps to reverse the process. Perhaps to change the process. Perhaps so I could survive the process easier than she.

To acknowledge that I can manipulate the English language is to tell my her-story or re-tell shimá.

To acknowledge that I can manipulate the English language is to say that my tribal language is scrambled within me. In my blood silently circulating. In my back pocket squashed incomprehensible. The color of my skin. The rhythm, ba-bum, the ticking, ba-bum, the map in my heart, ba-bum, leading me home.

My path predetermined by my blood?

That is the Diné will and spirit. And I am thankful I inherited this beauty.

First Light

In the beginning there was darkness. But by the time we emerged to the Fourth World, many things existed. Especially grandmothers. Shináli said prayer is part of our survival, giving thanks, manifesting our destiny. Many of the things given to us contribute to our survival, not because we deserve it but because our creator planned it.

I remember listening to the nasal low and high tones sounding like a chanter speaking powerful words. I would see the words flow over my body, tingling my skin. My recollections come from the instructions I received as a child. Instructions in the husky syllables of the Navajo language. Instructions familiar and natural.

Don't kill spiders, because they are your grandmothers. Don't kill horned toads, because they are your grandfathers. Rub one on your chest for good luck. Talk to your relatives and learn from their habits. Never be afraid of them. Never refuse food offered to you, especially if it's mutton. When butchering a sheep, all the parts are eaten or used to make rugs or clothing.

Know your clan. Know your language because someday only Indians who know their language will be recognized. Learn the ways of the bilagáana *but don't forget where you came from. To avoid bad luck, burn the hair that's tangled in your brush. Help shimá with the fry bread. Wave your arms over the fire and talk to it. Be careful of who you shake hands with when your parents aren't with you. There are werewolves about. Hogans are open in the east to greet the sun.*

Don't sleep late or the sun will strike you dead.

Facts

Born July 2, 1968, in Gallup, New Mexico, in the old Indian hospital on the hill. Raised urban among Los Angeles skyscrapers,

Mexican gangs, Vietnamese refugees, eating fry bread and beans. Middle child. Father from Birdsprings. Mother from Torreon. Daughter of Eddie and Susan. The U.S. Indian Relocation Policy placed them in boarding schools away from the rez. Five-Year Program at Sherman Institute, Riverside, California. Goal: annihilation of savage tendencies characteristic of indigenous peoples. New language. New clothes. New food. New identity. Learn to use a washing machine. Learn to silence your tongue, voice, being. Learn to use condiments without getting sick. Learn a trade and domestic servitude. Learn new ways to survive.

Whisper in Navajo after the lights go out. Rise early to pray.

Eddie and Susan, married 1963. Three children. Decided not to teach us the Navajo language. Two to three months of every year were spent on the Navajo Reservation. Definition: place where the sun toasts your skin with color from its painted desert after spring showers and the oozing silence thunders with your heartbeat. Close family. Always close(d). Fall 1982, freshman in high school. Shinálí died.

Went back to Birdsprings for two weeks. Anger. Anger for death. Anger for going back. Didn't go to burial. Piercing blade of random anger. 1985, daddy started getting sick, and his granddaughter, Alexandria, was born. Then daddy's grandma died. 1986, graduated from Earl Warren High School. UCLA or UC Berkeley? UC Berkeley. Daddy died on Wednesday, October 14, 1987. Withdrew for a year.

Anger. Anger from my sour heart. Anger at daddy for leaving us with no money. Hard on mom. Anger for his silence. Anger for giving me his dreams and desires. Transferring *victim* to me. My inheritance. Confusion. Changes too fast. Native lifestyle scrambled in assimilationist's mixing bowl. New patriarchal ingredients = no time to heal. Recovery is relearning. Returned to school.

Voice Inside

The amusement of the reservation never wore off, because there was always good fun: herd sheep, jump arroyos, ride horses, play BB gun tag, play card games. I never realized that those happy times in my life could end, would end.

Returning to California from the rez, I always felt different. Some sort of transformation had occurred, like visiting a mystery land. Spacious, almost no boundaries, I was free to roam, unlimited, freed from streetlights and cars and territorial gang warfare. The only limitation was mother natural, and somehow I seemed to break all her rules. I was constantly told not to touch this or capture that creature. I was unaccustomed to the mutual respect between people, the land, and animals.

The two worlds often clashed in me, creating blackness, a voice yearning to shout with boldness, the way my aunt used the Navajo language to get after grandkids or to tell a joke.

The rez has changed as I've grown older. Grandparents, like our land's vast beauty, seemed eternal. Aged with spirit yet never old. Animate and lively, never dead. Those relations shape the path my feet travel even after they've left this earth.

I look at *schicheii's* summer camp, trying to imagine shimá hauling water and herding sheep with my aunts and uncles. Two aunts and one uncle still live in Torreon. They are all educators, working for elementary day-schools. They deal daily with the trickle-down bureaucracy the Bureau of Indian Affairs passes on to Diné, then further down to local chapters. The economy of domestic dependent nationhood dehumanizes, re-invents Natives as chattels to be directed, displayed, and researched. As survivors of boarding school "education," a process of pure indoctrination and rigid transformation, their voices remain bottled.

The bottle containing the silenced voices hums. It hums old songs and whispers past lives. A sitting ghost, its coming unknown. I've seen the ghost. I can only ponder at the lore it contains.

In the summer of 1993, I worked in Torreon teaching creative writing to young people through Torreon Counseling Services. I was excited to obtain a job on the rez and a challenge to re-experience the place of mystery and good fun. Living there as a grown woman was worlds away from what I remembered as a child.

The population of our little corner of the rez was thriving. HUD housing communities had been built. More were in progress, creating some employment. However, most residents were not permanently employed. A small Thriftway trading store was still the closest source for groceries, gas, and video rentals. As a kid, the land was immense and magical. No matter how much skin and blood I left on the mesas and in arroyos, I continued to explore its crevices. That has not changed. The majesty of the land comforts the chaos that seeps down.

The rez is another nation, another worldview that functions in a space relevant only to the elements, strung together with language that also relies on the elements. The space is so specific that translation is impossible. My English voice and Western thoughts rival the small Navajo vocabulary in my head. TV and other media open a new dimension of crossblood simulation. Re-routing tribal identity with capitalist influences. Every little kid I worked with knew who Michael Jordan and Shaquille O'Neal were and how much money they made. Very few knew the name of our tribal president. In my generation and before, access to outside influences was not as disarming. Urban streethood appeals as much to rez kids as do traditional ceremonies. Our nationhood competes with itself.

I took on the responsibility of sharing my institutional knowledge with my classes. I exposed them to Third World writers, mostly women in the United States. My texts were the anthologies *Dancing on the Rim of the World* (edited by Andrea Lerner), *Making Face, Making Soul* (edited by Gloria Anzaldúa), *This Bridge Called My Back* (edited by Gloria Anzaldúa and Cherrie Moraga), and *That's What She Said* (edited by Rayna Green), and my own writings and videos. I confronted them with postcolonial thought from Trinh T. Minh-ha, bell hooks, and Gloria Anzaldúa. Key to translating Third World experience, these writers connect the dots, providing vivid descriptions of survival under colonial rule.

My students, as young writers, left me with the inspiration to continue writing and teaching. Since my position was not permanent, I was able to plant the seed of revolution but will never know how tall and strong the plant grows.

Sometimes I think the land has endured much better than my relatives. We have all gone different directions, and few of those directions have led to higher education. Three in my extended clan have completed bachelor's degree programs. Three lives have ended in alcohol. Many more remain affected and clenched by the spirit of alcohol. In conflict with our creator, the spirit of alcohol feeds off wounds acquired from centuries of genocidal battle. In a state of colonial confusion, the rez calls out to me to recycle and be cleansed.

I used to let my deep brown skin tint my image second-class. My nose narrow with a slight arc like the stoic Indian on old-time nickels. My skin glowing with red tones reflecting cedar-covered mesas. I see my image captured and bound in Edward Curtis photographs carrying water jugs from contaminated rivers. Biological warfare. But our creator is stronger.

$\frac{1}{4} + \frac{1}{4} + \frac{1}{4} + \frac{1}{4} = $ *Four Parts* $ = $ *My Whole*

Who I am is determined by my mother. I am Tł'ógí, related to Tódich'íí'nii, the Bitterwater Clan. I am the granddaughter of Pearl Toledo and Richard Antone. My nation is matrilineal and distinguishes maternal relations from paternal. The term *shinálí* is used for both paternal grandparents, while *shimásání* is maternal grandmother and *shicheii* is maternal grandfather.

I remember the fourteen or fifteen dogs grandpa acquired. The dogs were all sizes and all strays. When he took them in, they returned his kindness by guarding his dwelling and livestock. He had to kill only one for attacking sheep. I used to help feed the dogs the government-issued commodity instant potatoes. Grandpa rode a motorcycle to herd the sheep and had a blue-eyed / brown-eyed horse. Grandpa took us to his summer camp and told us stories about the painted desert's magic and the werewolf. He spoke English and talked in gentle and slow words. With the same voice he would sing Navajo songs.

Shinálí raised chickens and rabbits. She kept the chickens in a three-

tiered shed with a chicken-wire door. The rabbits lived in an abandoned station wagon. All the seats were taken out, and the rabbits made their homes out of old clothes and cardboard thrown about. She taught me how to gather eggs and chase rabbits. Sometimes shinálí would ask me to go into the cellar and get some commodity canned juice. The cellar was a mud-packed mound over a pit hollowed out of the earth. When I was little, I was scared to go into its cool, dark atmosphere. Shinálí stored commods and dried mutton in it. One year, a sheep's head rotted in there, and the stench of spoiled meat never left its depths. Ruthie Slick was shinálí's name. She was a small woman. Every visit, she would adorn me and my sister with jewelry. She used too much salt when she ate.

I still enjoy sitting behind shicheii's house, listening to the humming silence, storing the heat in my memory. The lazy heat melts your ears to the earth, and soon the ants begin to talk. Early in the morning, the Navajo radio announcer becomes part of my sleep, running free, jumping high over mesas, soaring with birds of prey. Only the country tunes played between bulletins stumble my journey.

Shimásání and I started weaving a rug together when I was ten. I never saw it finished. I was only reminded of it from an old photo. In the photo my hands are on the rug working and my head is turned toward the camera. The camera is turned downward toward me, and with my expressionless face I'm searching for guidance. Sometimes when I step into the coolness of shicheii's clay-walled house, I'll gaze at the photo hanging in a collage with other grandchildren's pictures. The photo was taken the same year I ate cold sheep stomach with shimásání.

Mom said we had to fight to get Torreon to be considered part of the Navajo Nation. Torreon is considered the Checkerboard Area. Shicheii remembers when our land extended out close to Albuquerque. Shicheii used to trade frequently with the Spanish in border towns and with other tribes in nearby villages, so now he speaks three languages: Navajo, Spanish, and English. My grandparents don't have birth certificates, but they have roll numbers. So do I. I was put on the rolls two years after I was born. My maternal grandparents are slowly withering away. I try to capture them on videotape, like the federal government, creating 2-D images that sit on shelves collecting dust.

I would like to document shicheii's life. He has seen many changes in the land, the boundaries delineating our existence, some years good, some bad. He has survived boarding schools, U.S. military service, shifts in tribal and U.S. government. He still tends his sheep, though the flock is much smaller. He's still active in the community, catching the bus to weekly senior citizen lunches and functions. In summer he follows softball tournaments to watch his children and grandchildren play in the sun. He takes his place as tribal elder and historian as he sips on pop.

URIs (Urban Raised Indians). We are city cousins. The ones who didn't know how to ride. Or jump arroyos. Sometimes it didn't matter if you were full-blooded because they knew you weren't from the rez. I was raised on a mixture of traditional knowledge and urban life. I used to think everyone ate fry bread and mutton. If you were Indian, you were Navajo. If you were Navajo, then both parents were Navajo. I had no conception of mixed-bloods. I thought all grandmothers lived in a hogan and could catch a sheep and butcher it, no problem. I did not know that being urban could be such a disability. A degree from UC Berkeley will never change the fact that I cannot understand my grandfather when he asks for more coffee.

My early childhood memories are sweet and are slowly coming back to guide my path. Other memories that I chose to forget long ago are also returning to guide my path. I don't speak Navajo. I feel it in my thoughts, flowing from my mind smooth as the wind. My enduring culture absorbed me unknowingly while I was playing with giant ant hills or helping to clean out the internal organs of a sheep. More than blood, my soul.

First Bite

The night before I graduated from UC Berkeley in the spring of 1991, I finally realized the gift. Being chosen to represent my classmates at our commencement, I was responsible for telling our story at graduation.

Every time I tried to write, all I saw were faces, not words: shináli at dusk, sitting, pushing up her wire-rimmed spectacles; my mother shuffling around in the gray hours of the day; me in the halls of UC Berkeley saying "Sorry" with my body as I move out of the way to allow others to pass; my father sitting in his armchair while I massage his shoulders. After dinner while watching the news, he'd massage his own feet. His body wearing thin from work.

So I wrote about him.

After my first year at Berkeley, he died, and I withdrew for a year. During that year off, I worked for the City of Manhattan Beach, doing clerical work full-time. I was making money and spending it fast, never focusing on goals. I didn't think about school until I had been working there for almost a year. My brain began to crave the challenge I had started at Berkeley.

I was readmitted the following year and began developing my writing career through the Ethnic Studies Department's Third

World Moving Images course, taught by Loni Ding and Robert Kaputof. This class enabled me to voice my concerns through the moving image. Once given the opportunity to re-create images, to re-tell stories, I used that medium to produce five videos and help found the Women of Color Film and Videomakers Collective. The creation of Native film productions is overdue, and the heart of good productions is the story. Someday I will put my story to screen.

As I began to write I thought, How can I show that my time at Berkeley was similar to my parents' experience in boarding school? The tension of skin color. People asking, "What country did you flee?" "What island do you come from?" The gnawing glare from the eyes of those who questioned my place in this country. Then, when people discovered I was Native, I was either ultracool or overprivileged. They assumed I received money and kickbacks from the government. Many of my classmates had no concept of Natives, especially those indigenous to California. With such huge cities as Los Angeles and San Francisco, many non-Natives considered themselves native because of the few generations their families had resided in the state.

There was no Native dorm or club when I arrived. There was no Native student orientation like there was for Chicano, black, and Asian students. I did not meet any Native students until my second semester in two of my Native American Studies classes. The Native American Studies Department was our Indian Center. That department was the contact with the surrounding Bay Area community and campus. UC Berkeley made it easy for me to be an activist because of its free-speech history and because there were few Native people on campus and little Native history in classes.

Out of a student body of 30,000, some 250 had registered

themselves as Native. The small group of us that reformed the Inter-Tribal Student Council often wondered where the couple hundred other skins were. As we began to investigate the list of students claiming Native ancestry, we encountered an alarming number of students who checked the box "American Indian" fraudulently, using the Native minority status to get into the university. Some traced their "American Indian" blood back many generations but had no knowledge of any tribal background. Some South Asian students from India were mistakenly checking the box. My outrage guided me to begin voicing my concerns early in my career as a student.

In the spring of 1990, Third World students congregated in thought and body to raise issues and demand a discussion of diversity among the faculty and the student body. Although the Native population was small, there was a push by other students of color to voice our needs. This thrust to participate physically was difficult, let alone the thrust to awaken a voice silenced for hundreds of years. My voice and the voices of other Natives on campus were not simply our own. We spoke the voices of our nations, our clan relations, our families. To tell or re-tell our story is not pleasant. And it is not short. It did not begin with the civil rights movement. It is not as simple as the word *genocide*. It is every voice collective. It is mixed-blood, cross-blood, full-blood, urban, rez, relocated, terminated, nonstatus, tribally enrolled, federally recognized, non–federally recognized, alcoholic, battered, uranium-infested.

Every time I was asked to speak, I didn't know where to begin. I always shed tears re-awakening old wounds in an almost-prayer of thanks for those sacrificed. I questioned my validity in that institution for higher learning. Was I learning weapons necessary for battle?

These emotions and questions rushed through my being. I had no examples from my family about battles in higher education. I knew only that injustices existed and affected my family. I knew my father and mother deserved more money from employment than they were earning. I knew we ate beans and fry bread over and over because meat was expensive and eating out was a special occasion.

I knew our state of emergency was valid.

That was what pushed me to the microphone. Every time I spoke, I knew I was more privileged than most Natives. Given the chance to voice. Perhaps change. Given the opportunity to witness institutional indoctrination. To see the process; to see injustice spill over the walls of institutions, splashing unknown passersby. My privilege was only as valid as my voice. I could legitimate our existence and need to survive tribally within institutions like UC Berkeley only when my voice, my weapon, had been prepared for battle.

The microphone that echoed across Sproul Plaza was true isolation. Standing before the hundreds who had gathered, who were waiting and willing to hear the words out of my mouth. Flashes crossed my mind, depicting our state of emergency—I would be in some border town standing in line at a trading store, negotiating ourselves for cans of coffee and sacks of sugar and flour. I would approach the gathered crowd with only my life stories, again wondering about my place in this student movement. How did I blend? How did I get talked into speaking?

Others would get up and talk about the movement and revolution and cite Third World leaders. I would be left out, trying to think of radical Native leaders who had said something to affect my life. Then I thought again and laughed.

Of course I never fit in, because the Diné philosophy and worldview were always considered radical compared to Western thought. Such a different means of approach and conclusion.

Thus my trouble with the movement. Many times I felt our goals collided. Many of the students, even the Third World ones, were middle class. The background of class was never discussed much, which led to many assumptions. To speak out and voice was easy for those with no jobs and noontime classes. Most never acknowledged the privilege of not having to maintain jobs and classes. The luxury of our existence in that university depended on our ability to pay tuition.

I was constantly reminded of my privilege simply by traveling home. I was awarded grant money to read literature and analyze theories of Manifest Destiny while my mother still worked two jobs. The irony always silenced me.

That day at graduation I began the way I was taught, introducing my clans in Navajo. Then I acknowledged that my language skills are in a foreign language, English. To acknowledge the use of an oppressor's tongue is to manifest change. All of us Native students were graduating from institutional warfare, fighting the dominant influence of intellect that presses realities of domestic dependency.

The university was pleased to have "minority" students as long as we remained the minority, silenced. The expansion of our minds in university facilities was explosive enough to curtail the movements we started to repatriate skeletal and ceremonial remains of Native peoples and to increase faculty diversity campuswide. The university stalled about commenting on our demands, hoping the issues would be forgotten, shelved.

With the strength of Native nations collectively, our resistance and humor, I graduated. Our stories, mutual, linked to bridge reinforcement. Our journeys, separate, unite to uprise.

From the Stench of My Belly

Sometimes there are experiences too delicate to re-live through memory, which often happens when re-told by the constructed and sinuous voice of nonfiction. Sometimes only the whimsical yet sinuous voice of poetry will suffice.

> this is me from me about me to those whose own story is
>   mutual
>
>   STOP
>
> i don't know when i realized the whole picture
> i know now that whatever happens
> our creator continues to give me strength
>
>   PAUSE
>
> my story is here and now and hopefully will discontinue
>   very soon
>
>   STOP
>
> others noticed i was different before i noticed i was different
> when i was younger all i was told to do was play hard and
>   rise before the sun

i tried very hard to follow those instructions

s l o w   d o w n   a n d   b r e a t h e   e a s i l y

i learned these instructions before i learned to remember

from my memory
i know how to pray
learned how to love
am here from endurance

my story is unique to my condition

*FLASH: DO YOU REMEMBER THAT PICTURE OF YOU AND YOUR
   BROTHER EDDIE JR., THE ONE WHERE YOU ARE TYING HIS
   SHOES?*

surviving in this place called the united states
is possible

impossible
for those who take it seriously

"if i was japanese
i would be a nisei
i am second-generation
off-reservation

my mother comes from
the land of enchantment
now also the land of poverty

drugs
illiteracy
and confusion

my mother
like many japanese during world war II
was relocated
off the rez
to a federally run
boarding school
in riverside, california, USA"[1]

my mother resides
angelic
among yellow-brown haze
indigenous and immigrant smog in los angeles
skyscraping progress pushing her home

*DO YOU REMEMBER IN THE DUSK OF SUMMERTIME HOW WE
    WOULD*
*MOW THE LAWN WITH DADDY, AND MOM WOULD MAKE
    POPCORN?*

i'm sure when you were young
your history books told you all about indians
or
i'm sure when you were young
you saw indians on TV
YOU SAW ME ON TV:
indian princess
rotund squaw

blood–thirsty brave
stoic chief
ungrateful drunk

*ONE DAY I WAS RUNNING, FELL, SCRAPED MY KNEE & THE
       BLOOD WAS*
RED AND I PUSHED YOU DOWN & YOUR BLOOD WAS RED

now
i'm sure when you were young
your fifth grade teacher couldn't tell you why

men worked on cars and built airplanes and school buses
men drank beer and played pool
they had friends named Buffalo Joe and Harold Jim
they laughed a lot and yelled a lot
and called white men chicken shit
men stayed at bars all weekend and wore dark glasses and sat
         in the back at church
their shame silenced and their anger roared you into an arroyo
safe from them and you didn't want to be like them
or know anyone like them
or love anyone like them
again

*MY FATHER WAS NOT ONLY A MAN BUT A HERO YOU WILL
       NEVER*
READ ABOUT IN HISTORY BOOKS

when i was young
i saw men as father

as a grown woman
i see my father
become me

sitting in a bar
silencing the war cry of my mothers corralled at bosque
    redondo
numbing the wound deep in my valley of cowboys and indians
recycling the memory of cold mountain fever

*DO YOU REMEMBER THAT PICTURE OF DADDY WITH DARK
    GLASSES
HOLDING UP HIS POOR TOURNAMENT TROPHIES?*

it is believed that my father was born in the year 1938
his birthdate has been recorded as october 23 and january 18
he was the son of ruthie slick, the daughter of marie tsosie
he was raised on goat's milk straight from the udder

*DO YOU REMEMBER SHINÁLÍ, HOW SHE USED TOO MUCH SALT
ON HER MEAT?*

my father was a southpaw
a stocky brown man
who loved to laugh
the game of pool
was his passion
he played doubles single-handed
a small-time legend at two-way inn

*DO YOU REMEMBER THE SOUND OF DADDY'S TRUCK
WHEN HE PULLED INTO THE DRIVEWAY?*

his face cool
reading the table
figuring out his next shot
settin' up the next dude
the next white dude
to give back
every time someone shouted, "hey chief!"
every underpaid job
every can of commodity food

ONE DAY I REALIZED THERE IS NO PAIN IN KICKING ASS

yeah i imagine him now
at every break
every combination
every clean shot of the winning eight-ball
i see him

yeah, my dad won
the game of survival
in a place some call the united states
in a country where memory slits your throat
he won

this is my story
starring the terminated mythic indian created
who still pukes up psychic trauma
remaining very much here in the homeland
recovering

SO HURRY, EAT SOME BLUE CORN MUSH
BEFORE YOU PUKE

Homeward

In the fall of 1992, I enrolled at the Institute of American Indian Arts (IAIA) in Santa Fe, New Mexico. Never before had I attended an institution of higher learning where the majority student population was comprised of Natives. This unique community has provided me with a safe house to re-cover, un-cover, and dis-cover.

Self, voice, and existence have all been nourished and battered. I have trained with instructors dedicated to the looming voices of new writers. Their commitment has brought in a series of Visiting Guest Writers, opening our small program to "established" writing communities. Within small student writing circles, I was challenged and amazed.

I am in the cycle of the whirl. The circle to complete my journey. A Long Walk, perhaps battling new giants. My path has been blessed with rich stories; my heirloom. With each pit stop along my journey, my collection of stories grows. The haven for emerging writers at IAIA is an inspiring working model. From the center of its skull, IAIA houses a furnace of voices, scrambled with signs of recovery, gagging on oppressors' tongues, a hope chest treasured with stories. From here I write. This point of trauma, twisting from depths of emergenc(y); hear, perhaps, listen with keen ears; our rage will transform.

The landscape of my writing will always focus on our struggles, from my memory, what I witness in my blood coursing through my veins, and stories overheard in bar talk. The will of my writing rises from shimá as daily as her morning prayers in the gray hours. The hunger in my writing feeds from my journey homeward.

 IMMERSED IN WORDS

Roberta J. Hill

The rhythms of life churn us like a great sea churns under a rising full moon. Wave crests nudge us toward shores we can't foresee. The rhythm of one wave resonates and helps create the second, third, and fourth until the circle of waves spends its momentum and jitters with other wavelets on the water's surface after the moon has gone. Life and writing share this common image. For every trough there is a crest.

We struggle, immersed in words. I grew up near an inland sea. Water, wind, trees, stone, and shorebirds have formed me. Some may claim that Lake Michigan is not a sea, because it doesn't hold saltwater and is neither large enough nor brackish. Yet if the Sea of Galilee, fourteen miles long, is a sea, then Michigan, more than three hundred miles long, is a great, shining sea. The indigenous people called it so. Such contrasts rattle in my heart when I see this earth and sky.

Each morning I take time to appreciate the place where I stand on earth. Intuiting the relationship between a language and the earth involves a struggle, for in dreaming and speaking I must believe in the power of language to capture my experience, yet I know that my vision will always push against the limitations of that language. Stories and songs live in the land. When we take time to feel alive on this earth, these forms of thought aid our survival by strengthening us.

I was lucky to be reared in a talented family and to belong to an indigenous nation whose traditions contain perceptive values, political acumen, and the pluck to continue despite difficult circumstances. I was lucky to experience the profound social changes of the 1960s and the 1970s, and to learn from remarkable teachers and friends.

The struggles Indian people face demand that we look for luck and then use it to extend our responsibility for creating harmony. I do not mean harmony in terms of leisure and comfort but the nurture of harmony within life forces disrupted by industrial civilization. The themes that give me the most energy are our relatedness and responsibility to this earth, the need for moral visions and transformations, the revitalization of ancient ways of knowledge that indigenous cultures of the world still respect and treasure, and the requirement that we rebirth our community life. All of these themes vibrate from the intelligence of the earth.

Oneida traditions remind us to feel gratitude for earth and water, grass and trees, animals and birds, air and clouds, sun and moon and stars. Daily gratitude gives joy and energy to our lives. Gratitude begins with breath and grows into song and story, for by breathing we exchange our life with the lives that help sustain us. By centering ourselves in the moment and tuning in to what is around us, we experience the earth's way of supporting our lives. By singing and telling stories, we harmonize the inside of ourselves with manifestations of the universe.

I find it impossible to look into the sea of my life straight on. It's a messy spot, full of cross-currents and doldrums. I take what I need from it as I go, but sometimes reflections return in amazing forms.

I've been many people, loved many people, and lived in many places, yet I consider Oneida, Wisconsin, to be my home. A year ago, I moved from St. Paul, Minnesota, to Madison, Wisconsin, and rented a friend's house in order to accept a joint appointment in the English Department and the American Indian Studies Program at the University of Wisconsin. Such a distance between my husband's work and mine brought its own struggles. My marriage to Ernest Whiteman ended in divorce this year. I have returned to using my maiden name. Love brought us into harmony for a time without my realizing how a union brings its own disruption. He still lives in the Twin Cities, creating visual art. Jacob, Heather, and Missy, the children we brought up together, live there also. When I look around me, I remember that the same earth loves us and connects us to our family and friends wherever they may be.

Outside the east bedroom window are budding trees and joggers on the short country road. Thousands of corn plants push their leafy tongues from brown clay loam. Robins, blackbirds, and sparrows chirp and chatter in the trees outside the window. To the south are two farmhouses owned by the families whose corn I greet in the morning. Two hills rise just beyond the houses. I greet them as grandfather and grandmother because they are old people, aware of and patient with our struggles. A row of white pines sixty feet tall edges the back of the lot. They swish and sigh, reminding me of the sea when I walk out the back door. These pines are an image of peace for Longhouse people. When I feel troubled, walking under the pines clears my mind and connects me not only to my personal past and future but also to the ancestors and the children to come. Beyond the western trees there are more farm fields, woods, and distant farms. To the north there is another field of corn, and beyond the field, the Stoner Prairie Elementary School, the fire and police station, and the town of Fitchburg.

Across the northeastern cornfield lies one of the housing developments of Fitchburg, with its rows of houses and duplexes.

Developers have left their mark in the way the houses are painted in standard colors of gray, ivory yellow, white, and blue, and shaped in rectangles and squares. Sometimes, when I drive through these houses to Madison and when I drive back to St. Paul and pass through other suburbs, I grow amazed by the wealth they represent.

Where does such wealth come from? There are so many suburbs with people who can afford to buy their own houses. Who are the people who live in such large houses? What do they do? What do they feel about this town, this land? Do they realize how poor most of the world's people are?

Neighboring farmers know that someday they will sell their land. Just down the road is an invisible boundary called the urban service area. City officials authorize which areas receive water and sewer services. Such urban master plans determine development. It seems that every year urbanization covers more farmland.

I like to envision the land before the urban nomads came. This land isn't Little Norway or New Tyrol. The Dakota, Kickapoo, Mesquakie, and Hochungra lived here, and they still do. President Andrew Jackson ordered the punishment of Black Hawk's band of Sauk and Kickapoo. After the encounter at Stillman's Run in Illinois, they fled the army and headed north to the Rock River. They stayed two months, and in mid-July the five hundred warriors with their five hundred women and children, all starving, attempted to escape to the Mississippi River. They were hunted and pursued by a military force of seven thousand men. On July 21, 1832, the retreating warriors fought Colonel Dodge's forces at Wisconsin Heights, near Madison. From Rock Island, women and children died as they ran or were made captive. Although Black Hawk tried to surrender to the steamboat *Warrior,* the boat fired upon the warriors, killing many. Reaching the river, one mother tied her baby to a lashed-together cottonwood raft, hoping that the baby would escape and find someone to raise him. The babies and children were killed.[1] No Moses found salvation in America's bullrushes.

Although Black Hawk and a number of women and children escaped, fear of retaliation led some Dakota, Hochungra, and Menominee to aid in their capture.[2] In 1830 many of Black Hawk's former allies feared they would suffer if they tried to protect their homes and villages. The result of the "Black Hawk War" was the ceding of eight million acres of land, along with one section east of the Mississippi named the "mining district."[3] Whenever I drive by Lake Monona or head west on Old Sauk Road, I reflect on their strength and their determined efforts to survive. All over Indian country the conflict over land and mining continues to this day.

The United States government has continuously worked to define and control its "Indian people." All the beauty and diversity of our ways of life are lumped into a singular American-made, tourist-trade arti-fact. When Native American people challenge imposed definitions, removals, forced assimilationist policies, and denials of our sovereign rights, an amendment gets attached to a bill to swing the pendulum of oppression in a different arc.

Just recently, a court judgment distinguished between "historic" and "non-historic" tribes. Sovereign rights could be upheld for an "historic" tribe but not for a "non-historic" one. Although the distinction was challenged and thrown out, it illustrates the ironic twists of Indian law. Some solicitors planned to define as sovereign only those indigenous nations who have remained on their traditional lands and kept their languages after five hundred years of genocide and ethnocide.

Historically, the federal government imposed definitions of "real Indians" in an effort to improve our living conditions, then it created the tools to diminish our existence. Such a process illustrates how Americans have distanced indigenous people from sources of power. Our identities are represented by irrational images formulated by conquest.

So destructive has been this process of assimilation and acculturation that some find it difficult to form an identity as a Native American person. Many of us pass through years of intense emotional pain, resisting our native culture's values and beliefs or believing we are not worthy and valuable human beings. We are vulnerable to self-destruction. Many indigenous people intimately know what Post-Traumatic Stress Disorder feels like because the process of being numbed to our deepest emotions and repressing who we are has been institutionalized within our cultures.

We search for self-protection within our families, clans, urban communities, or friendships. We avoid taking the risk of sharing our feelings and our knowledge with others for fear of being shamed. Such lateral oppression works very effectively to stagnate cultural renewal. For a culture to continue, each generation must grow within a way of life, work through the challenges presented to it by forces beyond, and pass the renewed values and beliefs to the next generation.

If we don't create, our cultures do not live. The need to create art and literature and music keeps our ways alive and nourishes them. All human beings need to feel the integrity of their own imaginations. Our imaginative life is another expression of the earth. Manie Boyd, a Menominee elder, once told me that to grow old and not to pass down what you have learned is a serious error, one the Creator does not excuse lightly.

As a child I felt the alienation and confusion of being exiled for opportunity's sake. Charles Hill, my father, served as a second lieutenant in the army during World War II. When he returned—

with Eleanor Smith from Flatwoods, Louisiana, as his wife—he attended the University of Wisconsin to study music and mathematics on the GI Bill. I was born while he studied. We lived in one of the quonset huts in a place called Badger City, built across Highway 12 from a monstrous ammunition storage dump outside of Baraboo, Wisconsin. When my father completed his degree, he returned to the Oneida Reservation, but there was no employment. He moved to Green Bay—ten miles away by car, light years away by heart.

Even after the Big One, the place where my father worked and lived in the old fur traders' city was still determined by the fact that he was an Oneida. Even though he had a degree and wanted to teach in a high school, he felt the sting of discrimination and was not hired. Even though my mother found a house they both liked and wanted, when my father came to close the deal, the realtor claimed fair-skinned bidders had bought it moments before. My father found a teaching position with the Wisconsin State Reformatory, and my mother worked as a nurse on the graveyard shift in several hospitals. My father kept his ties to Oneida and served on the tribal council during the years when the Oneida, like the Menominee thirty or so miles away, struggled against termination in the 1950s.

Both of my parents loved language and stories. My mother grew up on a farm in Louisiana in an area called the Choctaw Strip. If it hadn't been for the war, she never would have met my father, who was stationed in Shreveport. Her grandfather was Choctaw. At times she seemed to long for the less hurried ways of the South. "Go slow and easy if you want to get along with me," she sang. As we ate breakfast, she told us stories. When my mother died, I was nine. In that first year the house became her spirit, the curtains fluttering from an unpredictable wind that found me when I slept. My mother's passing filled me with loneliness. I learned how swiftly life can change.

My father was a musician and an artist as well as a math teacher. He raised my two sisters and me. In our house, music and art bridged our spirits, for he loved music as his father did. As a young man in the 1930s, my father played a trumpet in a band. When he was older, he played the guitar, banjo, and violin. My grandfather, Charles Abram Hill, played cornet in the Episcopal church at Oneida. He was a member of the Oneida National Band at the turn of the century. In 1892 he left Oneida to go to the Carlisle Indian School in Pennsylvania. From 1893 until 1905 he was on various outings, "learning" farm work for meager wages, most of his money going back to be saved for him at Carlisle. Lots of eastern farmers wanted Carlisle Indian "boys," although many, like my grandfather, were athletic young men. He returned with a love of baseball and modern music. He also returned with a wife from outside the reservation.

Dr. L. Rosa Minoka was a Mohawk woman, adopted and reared by Quakers. She was practicing medicine in Philadelphia when she met Charles Hill. She said of her husband that he played cornet "on every occasion and when there was no occasion." She loved literature, especially poetry. I felt a special kinship with her, reading both her medical texts and her leather-bound copies of Shakespeare and Longfellow. She knew about the struggle to learn and left our family the maxim, "Don't let school interfere with your education."

The lives of our ancestors still resonate in our own. We struggle with parenting because our parents and grandparents experienced a rift in their nurturing due to boarding schools and adoptions. We've been denied the richness of our particular families. Given the rigid castes in this country, some of the roots of my identity have been sundered by forced choices.

The definition of *Indian blood* is another ironic twist in federal policy derived from the divestiture wrought by the Dawes Act. The federal government recognizes my claim to be a member of the Wisconsin Oneida. I may choose to live among the Mohawk or the Choctaw, but because legal definition creates smaller and smaller pockets of indigenous people—and because clans and families were torn apart through war, disease, reservation life, and forced assimilation—I cannot trace those roots back to the families and clans. Some of our children, born of interracial or intertribal couples, cannot claim to be who they know they are, caught in the barbed wire of an either/or policy. My sister Rose Hill claims we're forced to define ourselves in one frequency instead of all the chords and harmonies of which we are composed.

The impulse for my writing was my need to find a way to deal with my anger. These days, I'm angered by the way lands on the Prairie Island and Mescalero Apache Reservations are being used as dumping grounds for toxic and radioactive wastes. I'm angered at the outmoded federal mining laws and the power of transnational corporations to pollute the ocean and the land with impunity. I'm angered that INMET, a Canadian mining company, shipped sulfuric acid by train from Arizona to northern Michigan to dump in their mine at Ontonagon, Michigan, five miles from Lake Superior. Due to the efforts of both Indian and non-Indian people to stop this, the Environmental Protection Agency is investigating the mine.[4] I'm angered that Indian people in America do not have religious freedom. I'm angered by the fact that we spend 51 percent of our national resources on the military, $868 million to investigate drug lords in Colombia, and 2 percent of our national resources on education. So many of the next generation of people, Indian and non-Indian alike, suffer from mental illness, drug abuse, and sexual abuse. The dominant culture is fragmenting into bits, driven by the force of individual greed. My anger is distilled in the writing, and the anger no longer harms my life but instead becomes awareness and social action.

I did not plan on being a poet or a writer; I simply love what words show me. I spent time reading books in what I thought was Shakespeare's garden at the local library. The formal garden next to the Fort Howard Library had beds for roses, pansies, and hedges. I performed solitary rituals there in fourth grade, sang to the brass sundial, and believed in invisible realms, in the Little People, in spirits. Children's books about them were not enough for me, so I read mythology, entranced by stories, trying to find a way back from the break between the living earth I felt and the narrow, closed, and rigid city.

I skipped along the sidewalks and railroad tracks of Green Bay's West Side, believing that angels and spirits carried me through the losses. Due to alcoholism, my world kept falling apart like the designs in a kaleidoscope. Just when things slid into a recognized pattern, with the blues and reds and greens glowing in a pleasing design, some force bumped the earth's axis and the design tumbled down.

My father and grandmother were Catholic, so I attended a parochial grade school. Some of the nuns were exceptional teachers, and I did well, especially because I loved reading and writing. But I learned also, when older students called me names and threatened to beat me up, that I was the Other. I was Indian, and they would hop around, making odd noises with their palms stuck

to their mouths. Older boys sometimes chased me. Such confrontations taught me to run very fast, especially down railroad
tracks. By high school I knew the subtle codes of social distance
created by racism and never dated, never felt accepted.

Doing well in school was where I found some pride. Years
later, as I reflect upon how that experience shaped my work, I
know oppression is insidious. The colonizing historians created
views about the history and values of Indian peoples and their
influence on American culture. From their perspective, Indian
peoples and their cultures were curiosities, objects of scorn, or
obstructions to expansion. I focused on studying, taking in poi-
sonous attitudes and beliefs but also identifying with rebels, car
thieves, and "juvenile delinquents." I wrote poems and stories for
us and about us. I sang to stay alive. I studied because my father
expected me to be a physician like my grandmother and because I
loved wordplay and languages.

What mystery exists in the rhythm, music, and images every
language gives us. I couldn't make clear judgments without the
thread of a melody tying together my emotions. The search for the
proper language, the one that matches feeling and intuition, keeps
forming in my life. But writing is not always a conscious choice, for
sometimes the words choose you and there is no other way to
handle a feeling but to speak, write, or sing of it. Sometimes it's
easier to understand as a story.

> Down this gravel road lived an Indian girl who
> loved a boy named English. She had known him since
> fifth grade, and he flirted with her a lot, showing her
> how exhilarating his bicycle could be when she perched
> on his handlebars. He had green eyes and black hair but

far fairer skin than hers. By fifteen they were both borrowing cars, careening over country roads, laughing and joking. They danced and dazzled and delved into life.

The boy named English was half-Irish, so he knew the proper ways and the ways to get around the proper ways. They could teach each other how to name what they saw. Her parents strongly disapproved, for they had other boys in mind for her to marry. But those boys had been exiled and lived in distant places. In fact, her parents had a difficult time even trying to arrange for her to meet one.

English showed her things. He loved the stuff, the goods, the hands-on boodle. He liked action, discovery, conquest. She liked dreaming the pathways of rootlets through the earth. She liked to smell the sand as she dug and gathered stones. He couldn't speak about dreams, where everything happened all at once. He couldn't describe how more than six people were related in a family. Her parents offered seventeen different ways to describe relatives even if they gathered in one small room, with three old ladies sitting down to chat and nine boys heading out to go fishing.

The girl grew older and her love changed. She thought life was good with English, but more often than she dared to say, she found herself dreaming of transformation. Whenever she tried to get English to talk about relations or feelings or energy, he slid into his chair, his eyes glazed over, and he got tough to handle. The Indian girl knew there were Others in exile, although she didn't understand why. She could see that English always ended up focusing on things. She pressured him and argued and shoved him when she could to make him handle those important feelings. He was hard to change.

After some time with English, she disliked his arrogance, his linear descriptions, his love of boodle. She hated the way he had kept other choices in the margins. He was always there, showing her his latest thing. She planned for the Others to join them soon. She is still searching for new ways to speak of relations, but English doesn't know it yet.

My father shared stories with us, teased us with allegories and wordplay. We traveled to Oneida to my grandmother Hill's house, which later became my uncle's, to the stone Episcopal church and mission, and to powwows, picnics, and other gatherings. My father told us stories about who we were as Indian people, stories of his childhood at Oneida, stories of his mother, who was a physician. He told us about the Peacemaker and the League, about how we had moved to Wisconsin after the Revolutionary War. Once my sisters and I received federal checks for calico. The checks were sent because Oneida people fed George Washington and his troops, who were starving at Valley Forge. Washington planned to send calico forever. It was the first and only check I ever saw.

Some poems in *Star Quilt,* my first poetry collection, reflect these experiences. I went to the university to become a scientist or doctor, but I graduated with a background in both literature and psychology. Peter Cooley introduced me to contemporary poetry. In his classes I felt more alive because poetry reaffirmed the energy of my spirit. He encouraged me to continue and to move to Montana, where I studied with Richard Hugo. Hugo empowered us in

the belief that writing is crucial to our survival in this world. Iron-
ically, he made us learn to trust our own sensibilities by sharing his
own rather overpowering presence.

When my father died, I threw myself away. I moved to the
Big Sky Country of Montana and a larger horizon. Whoever says a
mountain is not alive has not been alive in the mountains. The first
year, I feared them, but when I left I cried along the road down
Hellgate Canyon, not really wanting to leave. Both the mountains
and the people had become my friends. When I attended the
University of Wisconsin, in my last semester there had been thirteen Indian students. At the University of Montana, Indian students numbered more than 250. I was challenged to examine Indian cultures in new and profound ways, and in the radical protests
of the 1970s many of us gained a critical understanding of America.
I met and read the works of other Indian writers: James Welch,
Simon Ortiz, Leslie Marmon Silko, and Joy Harjo. The mountains
bolted me to writing and it was difficult to leave there and return to
the Midwest. I wrote in a poem entitled "Blue Mountain":

> I left that mountain easy in good-byes.
> The moon flooding me home. The Garnet Range
> like arms letting go moments
> when too much talk grows fatal.

Because of all the people I met and loved there, my writing life
expanded and grew in ways I could not foresee.

> She remembered then those three women who
> didn't know Idaho was so mountainous. They fol-
> lowed the other students from the university, heading
> toward the powwow at the Nez Perce Reservation.
> They drove half the night along the highway and then

turned onto a dirt road that only LeRoy and the other students from the res knew. By that time the three women were happily following the trail of cars on those dark mountainous roads, a long line of dust clouds and headlights and shouting as they drove one after the other toward the grounds. Someone had told them to stay close to the other cars. "You gotta take certain gates to get through, and even then you may not know just where they're going." Then the cars stopped and doors slammed.

There was no powwow. People walked down to a large, dark field and lit kerosene lamps. People rubbed shoulders and moved together in tight clusters of laughing faces, waiting for something. In the dim lamplight, the people looked beautifully boisterous in their search for the bones to play hand game. She wandered through them and felt the night and the mountain gather them inside its presence. Years ago in the mountains, she felt the joy of simply bumping into hundreds of other Indians who were talking, joking, snagging, toking, figuring out what to do if the bones never came. "What we need are those bones." "Who'd you say would bring them?" They never did.

So the three women left the grounds and traveled to LeRoy's house, a log cabin near a marsh in the mountains. They parked on a long dirt road under a tree and settled down to sleep in the deep night. When they woke up, wedges of sunlight lit up a large expanse of marsh. In other places along the valley, fog drifted over the ground and sheltered the birds, calling to each other in early sunlight. In that moment in a parked car, one woman found such peace. It sustained her for years.

The poems in *Star Quilt* also grew from my experiences on the Rosebud Reservation in South Dakota, where I moved after Jacob was born. Both places—the mountains and the plains—gleam like parallel universes in my memory. The plains helped me to understand the circumstances of our sorrow and our resilience. A subtle communion and communication sometimes take place between human beings and other beings on earth. In a green twilight, we took the cut-across from Upper Cut Meat to Spring Creek, and on the flat prairie road dust rose like a signal that we were headed down into the pines. Just then, as we slowed to drive the car over ruts and gouges, we passed a plum tree in the regalia of her fruit. She saw me. My confusion and my need. My grief clearer to her than to others I knew.

Years later, when I lived with Ernie in Eau Claire, Wisconsin, I had the same feeling—a wild plum tree looked at my life in its entirety. I had to stop on that autumn road and pay attention, for the plum tree at that moment knew my whole life. She knew more than I did about how to cross into the next world, to the next phase of life that I was beginning to enter.

In my second collection, *Philadelphia Flowers,* I tried to capture this in the poem "A Presence That Found Me Again, Again."[5] It is meant to honor those plum tree spirits that forced me to confront deep emotional truths in order to live.

Wild plum red as ever
along the river this morning I fade
from my thirties
Roaring across the flats ten years ago
I caught you glowing

in spite of my spume of road dust
watching me
little sun setting in violet leaves
bell ringing in the sea-green dusk
to one moving without moorings
to one singing as she sank
into dark piny canyons

Wild plum ripe as ever
along the river even then
you invited faith in feeling
offered me as sky when the sky gleamed
blue as my first mother's milk
buoyed me over swamp and coulee
like notes of a long lost melody
When I gleaned grief
you another reaper shook your red
skirt in leafy shadows

Wild plum red as ever
hanging on the warm edge of summer wind
the road mica bright
doors of sunlit haze
corn stubble
a gold procession against the shore
like long mornings before grief
I couldn't find my crossing
oaks trembled in their turning
smitten by that second most beautiful thing
we call death
I couldn't find half my life

until you held me
a tremulous ripple left
in your branches

and wind just awakening
for his rounds

At that moment I felt as if the plum tree had helped me endure my struggles and had given me the energy to go on. Most people have such experiences, but they are taught to deny them or to believe that in this material world such exchanges need to be ignored. So deep is Western culture's denial of a living world that we cannot easily share such experiences without risking being shunned. We're taught to think that only human beings possess intelligence. How hard it is to deny such an intense moment or many moments and find no way to engage in their profound meanings.

No wonder violence and emotional illnesses challenge Western culture. The dominant values complicate honest emotional relationships between human beings in order to insert a commodity mentality: I can't be listened to for who I am without the right clothes and antiperspirant. The same system also forces us to deny insights of believing in a universe at one with a spiritual intelligence. In a culture where all beings can be sold and exchanged and made into objects of commerce, all beings are imagined to be without consciousness, without the ability to share in human life. Even relationships between human beings are devalued in order to sell things.

The poem moved me to recognize the emotional interaction taking place between the plum tree and me. When we are open to the earth, the plants, clouds, rivers, and seas respond and gladden us. People feel a profound change going on: the transformation of greed into the need for recognizing and sharing our gifts. Not only are rain, stones, and trees gifts, but all the people we meet and love along the way are gifts. The most difficult to feel, within a dominant culture that wounds and devalues us, is the gift of spirit within each of us, a gift that treasures and honors our own creative power, a gift that acts upon the belief that our creative power must be valued and used in our lives.

I have been fortunate to learn from Jacob Hill and Heather and Missy Whiteman, the three people who have taught me so much about the struggles of this coming generation. My life has been enriched and changed from what it once was due to the process of being their mother.

I was fortunate as well to meet Ernie in 1979 in Washington, D.C. We had a dialogue about art and vision for more than fifteen years. His sculptures and paintings share the deep ties Indian people have to the living earth, and they point out the challenge presented to us as we watch industrial civilization around us pollute and destroy it.

Whether our struggle is portrayed in a poem or a story, in a film or a television show, or in visual art, we choose to struggle about how we conceptualize ourselves. Images we create as a collective entity will either edge us toward despair and apathy or unfold inside us and guide us toward the recovery of ourselves and the living earth. We already see and feel these images of healing. They wash over us like the waves, and we lend our energies to them because they appeal to us from the core of what we are as human beings. With struggle, we will create cultures that give people time to feel alive and to rest on the waves of these creative energies.

SEEDS

A. A. Hedge Coke

What would I be without language? My existence has been determined by language, not only the spoken but the unspoken, the language of speech and the language of motion. I can't remember a world without memory. Memory, immediate and far away in the past, something in the sinew, blood, ageless cell.

—*Simon J. Ortiz*[1]

When I was three or four years old, my father would sit me at the hardwood kitchen table with my older sister, Stephanie, and he would give us seeds and pony beads to string. I barely reached the tabletop, so I propped myself higher by sitting with my feet and knees tucked under me on the vinyl chair seat. The table was in the kitchen on the north side of the house where we were living in Amarillo, Texas, on East Eleventh Street, an unfinished road lined with clusters of Indian families.

The kitchen was lined with cabinets partly filled with flour, cornmeal, cereal, and macaroni and cheese, just like every other house nearby. The ceiling corners were crossed with cobwebs my father saved for blood coagulants in case we got cut or stepped barefoot on nails. If a spider happened out onto the linoleum floor, he scooped it up with his bare hands and carried it outside so it would be free to make webs somewhere else. The spider brought both pottery and weaving to people, my father said, and we should respect her for doing so.

Each time my father started us beading, I would try my best to get my stubby fingers to shape long, bright necklaces with corn and flower patterns. He would sit across from us and work on nine- and twelve-row patterns of his own. Once while I was still young enough to string only ponies, I finished a pattern that actually looked like what I'd planned. When I showed it to him, he looked it over carefully, nodded, and without saying anything about the beadwork, he smiled. Later he said my face was beaming.

While busy with the beadwork, my father would tell us about our ancestors. His voice was gentle and strong and had a rhythm that made it easy to remember things he said. It was rhythmically patterned, like a song. At that age the people we came from seemed to me like beads strung, patterned, and woven together into a whole people. The words he spoke to convey their lives, to give detail to persons who had lived before us, were like the shapes and colors of individual beads. Even old heart beads, where one color is layered over another, were those individuals with more than one side or purpose in life. What he didn't say—details about certain character traits and personal losses—was conveyed by obvious avoidance, by a raised eyebrow, or by a sad expression on his deep-brown face. This outright avoidance was just as important to us in learning something about our people as what he said. Maybe even more so.

I loved his stories so much that I taught myself to read by the time I was four. I believe I did this so I would never be without stories.

One warm day while our family was camped near a large lake in the Canadian Rockies, we kids were watching a palomino running with a bay. We wondered aloud why horses were colored differently. It was like a question contest between kids: "How come is that one yellow?" and "How come is that one brown and black?" My father was close by, and he walked over to make a story for us on the spot. The way he walked is something I remember vividly. He had a slow, easy sauntering way, as if he never was in a hurry for anything.

The story was about palomino and sorrel horses running

under pots filled with wodi—Indian paint—that had been hung high on tree limbs during Creation. He told the story exactly the way stories had been passed on to him by his parents, and he moved his hands to sketch out the way things happened during this coloring of horses. We were fascinated. The Creator poured paint on some horses, while others ran through paint spilled on the ground, speckling themselves from their bellies up, like pintos and grays. As we grew older, he added new colors and variations to identify the horses we were becoming familiar with. Every time he told the story it made perfect sense, and we loved it.

When I was older, breaking RCA and AIRCA roping horses in North Carolina for a cowboy named Jimmy Pleasant and swinging a riata and forking manure all morning, I would repeat this story on weekends to little ones hanging out on hay stacked near the stalls. Later, I was surprised to find this story published as a traditional tale. But as far as he knows, my father was the first one to tell the story. Maybe it shouldn't have come as such a big surprise. Good stories are repeated and shared so much that their origin becomes secondary.

One place we liked to visit was my father's oldest sister's house. Her name was Velma. She was twenty years older than he, knew all kinds of stories, how to garden, and how to make all kinds of things, including good food. Everyone loved her fresh bread and soup, bean bread, raisin pie, and her hand-wrung chicken stew with rice simmering in blue-speckled pots and pans. And, of course, she always had a big pot of coffee on the stove for guests and family. She was like a grandma to us kids—a hero.

Auntie Velma used to sit us on her lap and tell us funny stories about our family and scary stories of ghosts bothering people. She always told us to listen carefully, and she would laugh out loud if we got too involved in a story and questioned her about it afterward. She had an old woman's voice and deep-set lines in her skin to go along with it. Her hair was always pulled back, and she usually wore cotton print dresses. Though she was a small woman, her lap was soft. A feeling of comfort and safety surrounded us whenever we were near her, and the breezes sweeping throughout her open house felt like welcoming invitations from nature waiting outdoors. When we went outside, she would show us wild plants and foods we could eat.

Velma died when I was about thirteen. Her cancer wasn't diagnosed until she was down to sixty-eight pounds and already going home. I still miss her.

I am thankful Auntie Velma was still living when I was small. My father's father had passed on ten years before I was born, and his mother joined her husband while I was "on the way," so I never saw her. Once my father dreamed of her pointing toward me, her hair long and unbraided. Even though I was blue from asthma, he woke up in time to breathe me back to life. Because of this I was given some of my grandma's personal belongings, a corn stone and a beaded bag. Stephanie's hair is like our grandma's, dark, with one spot of red in it. She can barely remember dancing and singing songs with her when she was two or three. I wish I could have known her then. When I go home, I will.

When I was half-grown, I would visit older women in the North Carolina hills. They taught me to make baskets from ash, willow, and hickory, and pine needles. They showed me how to beat bark and wood until it was soft and pliable. I thought I was too clumsy to make beautiful baskets like the ones they showed me. Oh, how I wanted to make fine things, to be deft and clever. My fingers were slender, but my knuckles were stiff and my hands had too much tension in them. My first attempts at shaping baskets were pretty poor, but somehow I was able to improve my work with almost every new row of weaving. Before long, I got pretty good at the baskets, and I began to feel natural working with them.

In my early teens, a ninety-two-year-old woman who lived near Willow Springs showed me the way to quilt blankets. I called her Grandma, but her name was Maggie. I helped her too, by cutting wood for her stove and toothbrushes for snuff. These weren't toothbrushes like you use with Crest or Aim. This is what old women use to dip snuff, to place pinches between their teeth and gums. They were made from little pieces of hickory cut from the tops of trees, where the twigs are thin and fresh. It was a lot of work to climb the hickory trees just to get the twigs, but I was young and strong then. And I wanted to be doing things for Maggie.

Later on, when I was ready to work on my own quilts, my father told me how to make a quilt frame that lowered from the plaster ceiling of my tar-papered house to a workplace about three feet above the wooden floor. I left home in my early teens and had places of my own on- and off-reservation but always in the country. In each house I set up an area to work with fabric and a place to write. In my late teens I learned how to weave on a harness loom. I loved designing pictures and symbols in the weave and making fabric for clothes and rugs. I also learned to make mud pottery. After smoothing the coils down completely, I took shells and rocks and made patterns in the clay with their images. Today, when I think of writing and about the structure of a work, I think about those patterns, and I always think about the thickness or sparseness of the weave and the layers.

One of the things I really loved to do was to make cornhusk dolls. When we pounded dried field corn, I would gather up loose shucks. They would be stiff and dry, so I would dampen and work them until they were supple, at the same time cleaning off specks of dirt or insect flecks. After they were soft, I would fold, twist, and wrap the husks into dolls. Some of the dolls were shaped as I went along, and others I planned out. Sometimes I used corn silks to make hair. Sometimes the silks were wavy and thick, and they looked like real hair and added a lot to the personalities of the dolls. But I never put faces on my dolls. If I put faces on the dolls, I was told, I would be giving away something that should remain untold and imaginable. Each doll already had its own face, and I shouldn't place my ideas upon it. From this I learned the value of mystery and respect for the unknown.

I gave away all the dolls when they were done. I never sold them; they weren't made for that purpose. They were made for beauty and sharing. But I always made a story and a song for each individual cornhusk doll. When I wrote songs for cornhusk dolls, I often used hoofbeat and heartbeat rhythms to give the songs a traditional form. Within these rhythms were moods, tones, and emotions that reflected a particular shape or character I saw in the dolls. In making these songs, I learned more about songs and language, such as how repetition may induce a certain feeling, or relaxation.

You have to be careful about your ideas and thoughts when you make something, because your feelings transfer into your creations. Just as in nature, there is a resonance that must be acquired and maintained to propel the motion of events surrounding us at all times. In this motion, everything is significant.

In some traditional songs, tones have great significance, because they have certain emotional and psychological properties essential to the meaning and purpose of the song. In speaking a traditional language, repetition of words may also be used to emphasize certain things. For instance, *red red* may indicate that a material substance is red all the way through, or it could indicate a red pure in hue. Different words are also used to indicate different types of the same color—that is, words to indicate what a color is physically and what the same color is esoterically. And in the Indian language, nouns precede adjectives and are the reverse of what is expected and considered correct in formal English—*horse red* instead of *red horse,* for example.

Today, when I write poetry I sometimes incorporate Native ways of describing even while I am writing in English. This enhances the work and makes the writing both comfortable and startling.

My sister Stephanie and I wrote to each other with little chunks of sheetrock on the concrete slab outside our front porch. We used letters and pictures to get our messages across. Being a few years older, Stephanie knew more letters and words than I did, so she taught me what she knew and I improvised the rest. Sometimes we drew in the dirt with sticks or used burnt matches to make black-and-gray pictures. She often mixed food dyes and other stuff to make colors for our pictures.

I drew symbols to represent my sister, my family, and me. All over the cracked concrete steps, I drew birds hiding in bushes and clouds dripping with rain. We might stay outside drawing like this the whole day. Sometimes we talked; sometimes we just let the pictures talk for us. I always placed flowers, the sun, and corn in these pictures, like the designs we learned stringing beads. These were what spoke to me in a sense. I understood something about their properties, working off of what we knew of our family who came before us, from stories my father told.

My father's early life was humble, growing up in a dugout eight feet down and ten back. We thought this was normal and used to talk openly about this dugout. Other kids thought we meant a baseball dugout, and when they discovered we didn't, they called us "bucky and backwards breeds."

All my father's siblings were artistic in some way. Some painted, and some carved wood or stone. My cousin Lester still makes arrowheads traditionally. It takes about fifty thousand whacks, stone to stone, to get them the way he likes. I once saw him working on an obsidian point, and the air around him was completely lit up with black and red flecks. I could have watched him all day, but he ran me off, saying I shouldn't breathe the stone dust because it was sharp as glass and could cut my lungs up.

Lester's father contracted malaria in North Carolina, and he lived with it the rest of his life. He made beautiful silver-and-stone jewelry and handcrafted musical instruments. This wasn't unusual for my father's siblings, as they were all artistic. They were good singers or musicians at some time in their lives too. Some of my cousins still play music, and one makes a good living playing guitar.

My grandmother, my father's mother, was a traditional mid-wife. We were always told she was a very strong woman. She helped hundreds of women deliver their children, and she delivered her own babies herself. She knew what plants she needed to help her do midwife work and to help with common sicknesses. My father would make us teas from some of these plants, and he sang children's songs for us that she had sung to him when he was little.

One of my grandmother's own girls, Aunt Lucy, was born three months prematurely and she lived. Now she is a working rancher woman even in her seventies. Aieee, she is tough. The last I heard, she was chasing down a cow who couldn't calve. Once she had a stroke and only three weeks later drove more than a thousand miles to visit my father. My father says that when they were young, this sister was the authority among the children. What she said went without argument. I think Aunt Lucy was my father's hero when he was small.

Some years ago, four of my uncles "went on" very close together, leaving only my father and his oldest brother out of the boys. When Aunt Velma died, her death left two sisters along with the brothers. Both sisters are strong ladies, and we were raised to respect them for their strength as women. Rose left North Carolina due to extreme racial tensions. Schools were beginning to be desegregated, and the KKK came out in full force to prohibit Indians and blacks from attending white schools. Rose told us about the Lumbee Indians who surrounded those men in pointed sheets and yanked their masks off. She now lives in Carnegie, Oklahoma, where her husband was from, and Lucy lives on her ranch in the Pacific Northwest.

Despite having rheumatic fever in his youth, my father educated himself and worked all his life. He said that one thing that enabled him to get work was respect for communication. He said both sides of his family knew the importance and power of language. He and his parents could get by in various languages. His paternal grandparents were Tsalagi who spoke their native language and of whom we were especially proud because they came from devout holdouts who were against ceding any lands to the whites. His maternal grandparents, who were Huron–French Canadians, spoke many languages, including Cheyenne and Gaelic. This part of my family was against the colonialist English taking any lands, and they sided with the French, who were more interested in trading and marrying in. We were proud of them as well. No matter if we were mixed-blood, we were from people who did not sell out.

We were confused by my mother's family. We were told our mother was a prodigy who played classical piano and who was sent away to boarding school at age five. Her mother was directly from Europe, Sherwood Forest even. When we made pictures for this grandmother, she threw them away, saying they were too primitive. When our cousins, who came from her other children's marriages to full-blooded white people, made pictures for her, she hung them on her kitchen walls and told us how beautiful and sophisticated they were. I always thought that peculiar since she was a teacher who helped *other* Native artists get recognition for their work in Canada. Her husband traded horses and worked with Indian tribes. He never denied his Indian ancestry, but he did avoid the subject whenever my grandmother was around.

When we were grown up, our cousins finally told us that our grandfather's ancestors from Missouri were so obviously Indian that our grandmother never hung their pictures on the walls. Our grandfather was also of Portuguese descent, so it was easy for his wife to blame his dark skin on Mediterranean blood without having to accept the probably Muscogee side of him. My father raised *us* to believe that being Indian was what made us who we are— what *shaped* us. He had a strong sense of his own cultural identity and pride no matter how much ridicule he suffered as a result, and he instilled that in us. I think the problem our grandmother had with *us* was we were *related* to her and not out of touch with who we were.

It took a long time for me to understand my mother's mother. I hated her when I was little. I knew it was wrong to hate, but I couldn't stand the way she treated my father and us. It is still so hard to remember these things even though I forgave my grandmother long ago. I think this is when I first learned mistrust of white people.

I have relatives who have assimilated and who use the phrase "part Indian" to describe themselves. They hope to pass. My father said this denial dates back to vicious racism around the turn of the century.

Before the removal of the southeastern tribes, a contingent of hardcore Tsalagi led by Sequoyah went down to the Southwest—then Mexico and now the state of Texas—in protest of reservations in general. Chief Bowl also took a contingent and settled in Arkansas.

During the genocidal war on Comanches in northern Texas, the Tsalagi living in the area found themselves in grave danger. Many began to deny they were Indian. Their children heard these denials and repeated them. They live in what is now northern Texas and Red River County. Some of these relatives later married Comanche people. One of them has a grandparent who was lynched by Texans just two generations ago. Some married other Tsalagi descendants, and some married whites.

Today, it's some of these relatives who call themselves "part Indian" and sometimes still deny their blood in mixed racial company. When I was too young to understand this, I wondered what part they meant was Indian—the elbow, the nose, the knee?

While we sat and drew on the concrete, my sister Stephanie and I daydreamed. We imagined that great things would happen to us. We watched clouds blow shadows across our drawings, casting dark and light shapes onto the patterns, giving them an ominous character that became part of our own stories. Even though I possessed great imagination, I didn't have any way of knowing what would actually happen in my life, no way of knowing that when I was barely sixteen I would marry another mixed-blood, a tobacco sharecropper. And I had no way of knowing that during this marriage the fields and land I worked would become my backbone, stability, and balance, not just ideas and pictures formulated from stories, although these stories were important to how I was shaped and how I identified with the land. The stories laid the groundwork, so to speak, and when I was involved with it personally, the land became as much a part of me as my blood.

When we were making designs and pictures, I didn't have any idea that by the time I was twenty I would flee my first marriage when problems came up. Though the clouds shadowed our concrete slab filled with drawings, no foreshadowing warned me that I would fall into a relationship with a man who gave me a hundred times more stitches than he did kisses. Nothing foretold I would escape with only my life and my children and spend years far from the Carolinas. And during these changes in my life—on- and off-reservation, in or out of town, back and forth from somewhere to somewhere else—I would know that no matter how bad things got down south or back east, I could always run north to get back on solid ground.

I was born a dual citizen: Canadian on both sides of my family—native Huron mixed with French Canadian on my father's side and Canadian national on my mother's. I'm attached to the land there, just as I'm attached—because of my Tsalagi blood—to the land in western North Carolina and now to the land in the Dakotas where I have loved ones buried. So much of where you are from is in your blood. With mixed-bloods like me, it gets a little crazy that way. The good part about it is having more than one place. Place is important. Essential.

My father placed us with relatives while my mother received repeated shock treatments. She was put in huge concrete buildings. The windows were about fifteen feet above the floor, so there was no way you could look outside even if you wanted to. Most of the people receiving "treatments" looked like zombies, walking around in white gowns and slippers, mostly in search of cigarettes. I remember them pawing at us while we walked through to wait for my mother. Asylums were hard in the sixties.

It was also hard being mixed-blood. I always had to do the trading at the trading post because I was the lightest-skinned of the kids. It was viewed as an advantage because the dealer would assume I was mixed, and my family thought someone might even defend me if I was cheated too badly. By the time I was three and a half, I was competent enough at trading to barter for the other kids, and because I began taking care of everyday things so early, by the time I was thirteen I was taking care of myself completely. In my family, we were always busy trying to survive; we were always survivors.

Our family's survival skills were partly based on traditional agricultural knowledge. Each year, my father made a garden in the northeast corner of our lot—corn, squash, pumpkins, melons, and gourds. The garden was circled by flowers and other plants, like wild mint for tea. My father was very careful about the placement of the rows and patterns in the garden. We would help get everything ready. Once he gave the pumpkin patch to my sister Stephanie to tend. It had been her idea, and this was the first time she had a particular place in the garden to dedicate herself to. She was excited and worked hard.

At the time that Stephanie had the pumpkin patch to tend, our mother was suffering from severe delusions. We were too young to understand much about her illness. We remembered stories Aunt Velma told us and thought our mother was being bothered by ghosts who hadn't "crossed over" properly. The psychiatrists gave her so many shock treatments that her thick black hair was mixed with shoots of even thicker stark white hair, which would fall out. She was truly tortured and had a very hard time dealing with even day-to-day life. One day she began reciting nursery rhymes while she walked through the garden. She repeated lines from a rhyme about a man putting his wife in a pumpkin shell, and she began attacking the pumpkin row with a vengeance. A tall wooden fence stood along the northern boundary of the garden, separating our lot from the people on the other side. In great fury and rage, my mother began to hurl huge pumpkins over the fence, screaming, "Put her in a pumpkin and there he kept her very well!"

In shock, my sister quietly watched. The neighbor on the other side of the fence thought she was giving the pumpkins away and began gathering them up. He shouted his thanks to her over the wooden barrier. When my father came home, we told him about it. He said not to worry, that there were lots of pumpkins in the world but that we had only one mother. He explained that she couldn't help the way she was and told us to hope she would get better someday. He told us to be glad we still had corn to tend. From then on, corn has had a special place in healing for me.

I realize now that this experience gave me a perspective on the dark side of things. I try to face this in my work, to confront the issues that drive me, whether they are positive or negative. I believe this aspect of my writing enables me to survive hard times and hard situations by helping me turn harmful events around so they become something healing themselves. Surviving, always surviving.

Once when I was little I dreamed I was a deer, so my dad told me never to kill one. When I was older with kids of my own, living on the hills leading into the Black Hills of South Dakota, I had a dream I was facing a big buck head-on. I thought the time had come for me to kill a deer myself. The next day I went into Rapid City and borrowed a rifle. I waited high on a hill for the deer who fed near my place almost every night. The deer never came during the four days I waited for them. I was sadly disappointed and decided to take the gun back and forget about the dream. To my surprise, as soon as I returned the gun, the deer returned to my place. They munched on long grass right up to my porch, where I was sitting on the wooden steps. I realized I hadn't interpreted the dream correctly. I understood that I wasn't supposed to take down a deer after all. To this day I have never downed a deer. Sometimes, even when we have a dream, it may have a whole other meaning than what we have seen in its imagery.

The deer dream came while I was in mourning. I had lost someone to leukemia a year before. I didn't go to any social events or do any art shows or performances for a year because I didn't want to disrespect him in any way. The mourning affected my life and my life work a great deal. I stayed pretty much to myself, and when I was lonesome I sometimes went to the Wounded Knee Cemetery in the middle of the night to visit his grave. The tribal cops would come driving up the gravel road, shining their flashlights in my eyes, treating me somehow because I was in the cemetery late at night.

(I have to say something here. If you are Indian, you probably know what I mean when I use the word *somehow* above. If you are not, you may think I have made a mistake in grammar. I do make mistakes, but this is not one of them. This *somehow* refers to exactly how I was treated, since the cops assumed I was a troublemaker or drunk and treated me accordingly. We reclaim what we can by Indianizing even simple English words like *somehow*. This is part of

survival and adaptation. This usage may be referred to as a colloquialism, but it does not accurately describe the Indianizing of
English words and the English language. *Colloquialism* refers to
regional usage of certain words or informal oral speech rather than
the written form of dialogue. This description does not quite explain Indianizing, but I have to resort to the word *colloquial* to
convey what I mean about this use. I find this frustrating but necessary. After this digression, now I can continue.)

The cops really made me mad. I was praying in the cemetery,
visiting a loved one, and they came harassing me—at least, that's
how I saw it. Yet I couldn't get mad, not right there next to the
graves. I would have to excuse myself and meet them under the big
arch at the entrance to the cemetery. Then get mad. I felt like riding
over to the KILI radio station and requesting the song "I Shot the
Sheriff," dedicated especially to those guys. They made me mad
because I really had nowhere else to go with what was on my mind.
It didn't involve anyone other than the one who had crossed over. I
just wanted to spend the year of mourning in a respectful way so
that I would be able to let go when the time came. But those cops
wouldn't leave me alone; that's why I was so angry at them.

When we grieve, we are told it is important to go on with
our own lives—for the living *and* for those who have gone on—
even though we may feel like we don't want to. It's good to pay
homage to the lost one by creating a song or something to give
away after the mourning comes to an end. After the year ended, I
went back to school, to the Institute for American Indian Arts in
Santa Fe, and I wrote a piece for the loved one who had gone on. I
wrote it partially in his tribal language as a tribute to him. I know
enough of the language to have unconscious thoughts in it, and I
couldn't have written the piece in any other way.

Writing the honor piece enabled me to complete the process

of grieving and to let go. This was the responsible thing to do. Although this was not the first death that was close to me, it was significant to my own development and to my work. I was devastated by it for a long time. Experiencing this loss matured me in certain new ways, and this grieving helped me to find a more developed sense of purpose and to continue to develop spiritually.

When I began school, I started in the first grade because we didn't have kindergarten or Head Start. I was late to school every day because my mother would have things for me to do. She was sick at the time, and it was important to take care of what she wanted done before I left for school even if it meant scrubbing the painted baseboards with a toothbrush. Every day I would get into trouble as soon as I walked into class late. My teacher would demand to know where I had been. I would say nothing because I didn't want to talk back or say my mother was sick and needed me to do things. I didn't dare look at the teacher's face. At home we understood it was rude to look directly at people's eyes, especially during a scolding. The teacher said I was lazy and belligerent and sent me to the principal's office every day.

When I got to the principal's office, he said I was bad, and for my tardiness and my bad attitude he hit me with a wooden board with holes drilled in it. The holes made my skin rise into blisters where the board landed. But no matter how hard or how many times the principal hit me, I did not cry. I took the swats and did not tell family secrets. I took all of this and never cried once. I also did not tell my father what was going on because I was ashamed of being a lazy, belligerent, bad girl.

I continued to do housework and other chores when my mother asked, and I continued to be late and learned to put up with rough treatment as a part of school life. I learned I was bad and needed to be punished, and I learned not to cry. The only way I could have some control over the situation was to shut down the part of me they wanted to punish and protect it from them the only way I knew how.

When my father was in school, his teachers had beaten his hands so badly that he developed early arthritis. His mother's grandmother was the first member of our family ever to be taken to a boarding school in the province of Quebec in Canada. Her family and other families repeatedly brought canoes up the river to take their daughters back to the village. The girls would all wait for the boats at a certain place on the riverbank. The French nuns were hysterical about the loss of their students. They demanded their return, and the girls were always taken back to school. By the time their schooling was over, the girls had changed so much that their families mourned for them as if they had been lost forever.

That was a long time ago, but even today my sons have been called belligerent and rude for not looking up at their teachers during a scolding. They have been ridiculed by teachers for climbing trees and for eating wild mint. Despite federal legislation like Johnson O'Malley and Indian education programs that are designed to help schools understand cultural differences, such harassment still occurs. When my older son was in the seventh grade at St. Catherine's Indian School, another child was constantly harassing him because his hair was past his hips and braided. The other child's hair was "clean-cut," and he came from a devout Catholic family who donated large sums of money to the school. The principal even joined the other boy in harassing my son, saying he was doing this to "toughen him up." Older kids from the school called me at home to tell me what was happening, and I got to the school in time to witness some of this harassment. Here was my boy high in a tree and being teased by a bully and the principal. All I could do was to pull him out of school for the remainder of the year.

One of my son's teachers, who was new to the school, filed complaints against the principal and quit her job. I think she may have been the only teacher who was not a nun. Not all the nuns were unkind toward my son; in fact, most seemed genuinely to care about him. But one of the nuns constantly told me that the other boy was a "good Catholic," and if my son would just study harder in theology class, he might understand why he had a hard time with the boy. The same nun also said she thought that since I was a single parent, my sons would naturally be shunned by other boys with two parents.

The boy who started all of the problems was never reprimanded, but he quit school before final exams. Afterward, the principal called to say my son would be allowed back for final testing if I wanted him to return.

My children can tell me what happens in school so that I can help them. But because of what they have gone through, because of what I went through, and because of what my family has gone through in schools, I do not want my children to go through unnecessary punishment and the systematic breakdown of their sense of self-worth. In the traditional way, our children were never neglected or made to feel shame because of the status of their parents. Children were celebrated, respected, and honored.

With the dominant society forcing new philosophies and shame upon us, things have deteriorated. An excellent film by Native people of Alkali Lake in Canada shows how this process originates with boarding school policies of assimilation, which force children away from their true culture using beatings for speaking their language, abuse by non-Indian adults who are in charge of the children, the encouragement of a feeling of shame for being dark-skinned or for having a different way of praying and believing, and the introduction of concepts such as illegitimacy.

I don't understand how a child can be illegitimate. A child is flesh and blood, and he or she was conceived by a woman and a man. Regardless of the relationship between the two parents, the child exists; he or she cannot be illegitimate. Illegitimacy is simply a concept designed to control and to persecute innocents. It is a barrier to natural expression, to enjoying life free from unwarranted guilt. When we have new or culturally different means of expression, we are often told that these ways are illegitimate. To a child this means his or her work, creativity, and cultural expression are illegitimate. The concept of illegitimacy is applied to things that are outside of the European philosophy of what is correct, of what works for European or Euro-American philosophies and practices. As those of us classified as Other develop what is correct for us, we must challenge this theory and code of ethics.

I enjoy reading poetry and prose with layered imagery. Some of my favorite writers are Joy Harjo, Linda Hogan, Zora Neale Hurston, Maxine Hong Kingston, Ursula K. Le Guin, Leslie Marmon Silko, and Luci Tapahonso. There is a certain pattern in each of these writer's works that is continuous and compelling. In my own writing I hope to use words in such a way that the images build upon each other in a fashion not unlike patterned cloth or quilting. For instance, when I am concentrating on plants or flowers, I try to create within the words a shape that is living and growing. This might not be an actual physical shape on the page, but it would be a shape created by the resonance or images within the words. I like words to have movement and dance within themselves. I like words to breathe as if they were flesh and had life within them, to speak for themselves.

I used to tag along after my father and watch him do things during the day. He was always busy with some project, and some of the things he did made me curious. One day I asked him how he carved wood into figures, and he told me, "You don't carve wood into figures, the figures are already in the wood." He held up the half-finished wooden dog he was making for me and said, "You free the figure by cutting away whatever doesn't belong to the shape of the figure." I have always wanted to free the shapes and images I saw or imagined in order to communicate them.

There have been times when my relatives and others have asked me to speak for them, and at those times I did. When I was still young, I accompanied my father on business and bargained at B and D's Trading Post. Ten years ago I represented our family at the Red Clay gathering. And there have been many other times I have represented people while working for Indian organizations on a national and binational level. In the back of my mind, I always have the words of my father telling me, "Don't speak unless you have something to say," and "Always remember what you do know." Now I speak for myself, but I carry the teachings of my father, my aunties, and my grandmothers, and I carry the hope for my children and their children's future. By sharing what I have to give, I hope that something can be accomplished and that a benefit will result from the exchange.

For me, sharing is integral, but there are things we must have respect for and protect at all costs. For me, the things I do not believe in sharing are usually those that are in danger of exploitation. I will not share traditional spirituality or cultural and intimate family secrets outside of the place of origin. I will not share what has special spiritual significance for me, my relations, and friends. Some people may be offended by this and by my need to write in a language other than English without convenient translation. It is not my intention to offend, however. Perhaps the piece is intended specifically for the people who speak the language it is written in. I do not think I necessarily write for the non-Indian audience, though I do hope my work can be a catalyst for understanding in some way. For similar reasons, *I refuse to italicize words written in Indian*. I believe italicizing words causes them to appear garish or cartoonish, or a caricature of what they are.

Sometimes non-Indian people tell me they know only one or two Native writers' works. Not coincidentally, these are writers who happen to be writing specifically for a non-Indian audience. I hope someday this situation will change. Whether or not a Native (or mixed-blood) writer is writing specifically for the non-Indian audience, the best work is vital and important to everybody. In fact, the more rooted people are in their own community, the more likely their work will lead there.

A good example of this cultural rooting is evident in the work of Luci Tapahonso, the Diné poet and writer. Tapahonso has a soft but no less strong way of working words into the best shape for her intention. She cultivates a beauty in words that create a suppleness in tensions of poetry and prose. Tapahonso is a weaver of tales. Her storywriting and narrative work carry the flair and cleverness of a great storyteller. She brings the reader into the scene easily, immerses the reader in subject matter and content, and then returns the reader to a pre-established place of grounding (often where she began).

Tapahonso has perfected this timeless manner of involving the audience in the material, and it remains successful and works well for her. Two of the most compelling aspects of her work are her sense of culture and place, and her well-honed method of bringing the reader there. Her work shows both beauty and intelligence. Her poetry and prose show a maturity in voice and syntax. I think the prosody found in her work is brilliant. Though I do not believe that Tapahonso is necessarily writing specifically for the white audience, I think her words are a great gift to the entire literary world.

I began writing when I was young. I felt I had to write, to create. It was more of a compulsion than an intellectual choice. Writing gave me a point of focus and peace of mind. It helped me to endure and survive, and it still does. I feel lucky because I have always cultivated the writing even when I was really young, when I was being shifted around from relative to relative to avoid being lost to the system, to avoid being placed somewhere that there would be no blood ties.

Each time I sit down to work, I am moved by the patterns in my life and by the patterns shaping my relations. As I said earlier, the people we came from seem to me like beads woven together, patterned and woven into a whole people. These people are always with me. They are a part of me. They lend an unseen hand in everything I do. They help shape the work by what they did in their own lives, and this I must remember to do with my own life, to give back to future generations what was given to me.

All creative work feeds other creative work. The memories I have imprinted in my mind from making bark and pine-needle baskets and from weaving fabric are significant for my writing today. These weaving skills may produce layered imagery, a tangle of raw material shaped into something tangible through gentle strokes of the fingers and the mind's eye. Working clay into pottery gives a certain strength to the creative flow while it makes the material more concrete. It also keeps the earth close, grounding the work. Patterning also appears in hunting and growing foods, a growth and survival pattern that helps the writing develop into something accessible, sustaining, something to feed the creative spirit.

I come from a long line of storytellers, from people who appreciated language and communication, from people who enjoyed life no matter how poor or alone they were. No matter where we were or what we were doing, we always knew where we belonged and what made us who we were. We always understood the effect of blood ties and cultural sensibility. We always understood the importance of the struggle to survive, to resist the effects of outside forces, to prevent them from stifling our ways and our creativity. This is the work, the legacy, the means for continuation.

HOW MY GHOSTS GOT PALE FACES

Daniel David Moses

My first play, *Coyote City*, began in darkness.[1] Then the voice of a man said:

> Give me a drink. I need a drink. Shit, I'm over here,
> you bugger.

Then a light came up, letting the audience see that he was a young man, an Indian man.

He continued his monologue, talking to someone who, it seemed, stood just beyond the light:

> I'm almost empty here. Come on and dispense with
> the booze.

> Please man, I'm good for it. You can trust me. I'll pay
> you tomorrow first thing. Come on. Come on, man,
> really.

> Hey, you want my knife? It's a real beaut. Look at all
> the things, man, the gadgets. Hey, you can even cut
> your toe nails. Come on, guy, just one more beer. Shit.

> Hey, how about a date with a real doll? Shit man, she's
> fresh from the bush. I'll give you her number. Real

pretty Indian chick. What do you say? What do you say?

How about a story my Grandad told me? A real good story, man. A love story. Come on, man, the ladies really love to hear this story. Shit, it gets them all loose. You like loose ladies, don't you? Just another beer, man, just one. That's all.

The first time I got invited back to my alma mater—Vanier College of York University in Downsview in the northwest corner of metropolitan Toronto—as an honored artist, I read from this piece, and one of the students, a fair-skinned, dark-haired young man, asked me whether I thought I was exploiting stereotypes of Native people. He sounded angry.

I was surprised by his reaction.

It was as if he hadn't heard my introduction to the piece, as if he hadn't heard the whole piece itself, had heard, say, only the section I've just shared with you.

My introduction explained that my inspiration for *Coyote City* came partly from a story my friend the poet, storyteller, and children's author Leonore Keeshig-Tobias had come across one day in her reading and had shared with me. It's a story from the Nez Perce called "Coyote and the Shadow People," in which Coyote's love for his deceased wife is almost strong enough to bring her back to life, almost good enough to guide the pair of them across the barren lands between the land of shadows, the land of the dead, and this world of light, where people like us all live.

Since it is a Coyote story, my introduction emphasized the "almost."

I also probably told those students how I had known I needed to do something with the story, write something, how I had to find my own way to tell it, that something in me knew how important that journey to the land of the living was even when I was first reading it. I knew it was beautiful.

My introduction would also have admitted that it took me a long time to find my way to do that, partly because my everyday world of part-time jobs and subway rides took up a lot of time (I was working security at the Art Gallery of Ontario) but mostly because I felt the distance between the archetypal story of love and death and my everyday world seemed too great a journey for me to make. How do you connect an eternal truth with dry-cleaning receipts? How do you bring the land to the city?

My introduction may also have mentioned that it was one of my favorite people, my sister, who happened to push me into making my first few steps along the path of that journey.

She lives in another city and was then associating with people who I felt had an unhealthy interest in what the tabloids call the paranormal. One day in October she telephoned, and after reminding me with her characteristic bluntness that her birthday was approaching, inquired whether I might like a suggestion as to what her present from me might be.

What she wanted was a book, which pleased me, because she's not been much of a reader since she got out of school, much to my professional chagrin. The one she requested, however, was whichever book Shirley MacLaine had just released. And she wanted the hardcover, didn't want to wait for the paperback. So I found myself down at the local occult bookstore buying it for her, feeling vaguely embarrassed but also reasonably sure that no one I knew would see me there. As I stood in line with the MacLaine volume in hand, waiting to pay, there on a shelf of books beside the cash register I noticed the title *Phone Calls from the Dead.*

Yes, there was an entire paperback book composed of anecdotes gathered from hundreds of people who had heard from someone from beyond.

The image of a phone call from a ghost became my direction into that play. How clearly it made the connections I needed for that long-distance call from the city to eternity, for that return ride the characters of the play take from the land to the now. Suddenly it seemed so obvious and true to me, this extraordinary experience that all these regular people knew.

Of course, in my own head, I admit, I kept using the term *folklore,* as if what the folks, what people know, shouldn't count for much.

Telling that story there in the bosom of my university, I may even have taken the opportunity to point out that my having spent six years getting a higher education, even if it was more or less in the direction of the fine art of writing, had not really prepared me for dealing with what could only be described by my university-trained rationality as irrational.

I doubt that my introduction would have admitted that my dilemma at the time was that this lovely story that had me in its grip was in essence a ghost story, and that I knew that we all know that ghosts, well, they just don't really exist, do they, at least not like they did back when we didn't know science. Don't we share a different reality now?

Somehow I wasn't quite ready to accept what any educated person would see was only anecdotal evidence.

No, I wasn't at all ready to accept the story.

I did admit to myself that maybe my heart was sort of possessed by the "spirit of the story," but in my head, for too much of the time it took to develop the play, I kept using the word *metaphor* as if a literary label could control this edge of reality.

It didn't much help that the first director I worked with on the piece directed the actors' attention to each scene in which the ghost appeared by singing the theme to *The Twilight Zone*.

I wish now I'd been confident enough to mutter to her something like, "I bet you never get to direct *Hamlet*."

But metaphors don't talk, so I had a hard time writing until I made one of those imaginative pole vaults student writers are always encouraged to make, using as a pole the rationale that the ghost in my play was just another character, just a regular guy, a human creature who had to deal with a handicap: being dead but not realizing it.

Thus did I first cautiously touch down in the land of the dead, assuring myself that the land was merely literary.

Yes, I had spent all those years schooling my heart to write, and my head still thought that stories were unimportant!

But in that land that I insisted was merely literary I made or met my first ghost.

But I'm sure my introduction to my reading included none of that worry, only a slightly ironic apology that I had to give away one of the play's little surprises because, practically speaking, there wasn't time for me to read all the way through the play to the scene that revealed the truth about Johnny, the young man wanting the drink—that he's that ghost.

And what better explanation could there be for his ability to look through the "fourth wall," usually so impenetrable to a dramatic character, as he continues his monologue? He'd failed to get a drink from the unseen bartender, so he turned from that light to the darkness where the audience sits and addressed them with the following:

> Acting like I'm not here, like he can't see me. Acting like I'm just another drunk Indian. Think he thinks I've had enough? Do you think that too? Do you think I've had enough? Enough. Shit. You think I've had too much. Well, who the fuck are you anyway? I don't know you. I don't know you. Shit, you're not even real. I know I need a drink when I meet you. I look at you and I need a drink. Hey, you're nothing but a bunch of spooks. That's why I got the shakes. You're the ones took Coyote in when he went looking for his woman. But no way you're tricking me. No way. I'm too smart for you. You can't get away with all that stuper-shitting with me. You're not going to get away with anything with me. You're going to buy me a drink. Shit ya, you're going to buy me a fucking drink.

The fair-skinned, dark-haired young man had listened but had not heard all those words and somehow also did not appreciate the myriad ideas that the theatrical context I'd created implied.

I'm sure I replied to his question about stereotypes in the negative, at least in the sense of exploitation being unethical.

I probably pointed out that using stereotypical images was one of the strengths of the theatre, that when you have only an hour or two to get your story told, you often have to start with the vulgar, easily recognizable version of things and then do your best to try to shift and enrich it.

Didn't he think that by making the audience face the "drunken Indian" right at the start of the play I'd get their attention and some of their emotions engaged? Wouldn't the play, by later redefining that character as one of the dead, suddenly be able to turn their heads around even a little bit? The city of Toronto begins to look a lot like the land of the dead! What are these people, my characters, doing there?

I thought I had created a veritable *coup de theatre*.

But the fair-skinned, dark-haired young man just sat there through the rest of the questions, and he still must have been angry, dissatisfied with my aesthetic rationalizations, because he left the room immediately afterward rather than staying to share the free meal the master of the college and her students had prepared, which is not what I remember as rational behavior for an impoverished student.

At one point in the conversation over the lasagna, the master, in an aside, apologized for the young man. She told me that until quite recently he'd been in the dark himself about his own roots and had been told by his adoptive parents that his biological mother had been a Native woman, probably Ojibwa. He was very sensitive now about Native issues.

I bet I laughed one of those laughs you get when you start to understand something that puzzles you, when irony is sharp and clear, when the present suddenly connects with history and you feel momentarily sure about what you're doing now and about your future.

It's hard to see around anger.

I wonder whether, if I had known who he was, who he'd so recently become for himself, I would have been able to tell him what he needed to hear, alive and suddenly alone there in the halls of academe, uncertainly Indian despite his fair skin?

Saying, "It's just a play. Don't let it bother you," or suggesting that the character wasn't necessarily him or me—"You're not looking in a mirror!"—but just a spin on a stereotype, just a metaphor, a probe into a problem, no longer lets me feel smug.

But I was still glad my "drunken Indian" had upset him—and surprised that it had hurt him. Other, older Indians have grown tougher skins.

I hope I could have taken him by the hand, given it some version of the shake, and said with sweet, clear irony something like, "Welcome to the race."

I hope my work would finally have encouraged him, raised his spirit.

But in my memory now, he's still fair-skinned, dark-haired, young, but lost like Johnny, my besotted ghost, in some city, not knowing who his people are or where they come from, not even able to be one with that mixed bunch of people who appear as the audience in the dark theater, both wanting to get spooked and afraid of its happening.

Since *Coyote City* was produced and published, I have met so many audience members and readers who felt free to tell me their own personal ghost stories—real experiences that can most easily be described or explained as seeing ghosts—that I've had to admit that I don't really know what we all know. I know now anecdotal evidence is not unuseful. Yes, I think I'm both envious of those experiences I haven't had and strangely satisfied that there are many things in this life about which I remain in the dark.

Perhaps it's that lack of actual experience that allows me my virtual reality ghosts, my theatrical spooks. I can keep on using them as directions, as probes into my own perceptions, my own quandaries.

The ghost is one of those recurring, even haunting images that keep coming into my plays. It seems to be a part of what makes

my work work. Even when the image of the ghost is not specifically present, there's always something or someone whose very
absence is itself part of the play's process.

Maybe the ghost is doing much the same job for me that
Coyote does in all the old stories.

While *Coyote City* was running at the Native Canadian Centre of
Toronto back in June of 1988, I met another fair-skinned, dark-
haired person. She introduced herself as the artistic director of
a small theatre company that produces work for young people,
mostly pieces based on European fairy and folk tales but done up
with a lot of ballet and modern dance.

She had already had some success with an adaptation of a
West Coast tale about Raven stealing the sun, and now, enthusias-
tic about my work, she wondered if, for instance, there might exist
an Indian version of a story like "The Sleeping Beauty" that I'd be
interested in dramatizing for her company.

My first thought was, not likely.

I grew up on the Six Nations Reserve, a mostly Iroquoian
community on the Grand River lands in southern Ontario. Anthropologists have chosen to describe our traditional culture as
matriarchal. Even though a large part of our population has been
Christian for centuries and a lot of our traditional cultural forms
have changed, a lot of our values haven't.

So I couldn't imagine even the Christian women I knew
when I was growing up there acting like a princess and taking a lie
down to wait for some man to solve her problems. Sometimes I
think the women think we men *are* their problems.

So I told the artistic director no, and I suspect she was disappointed that the Sleeping Beauty story wasn't one of those univer-

sal stories we've all been taught to look on as the great ones, but then she herself, the head of a theatre company, wasn't what anyone would call a helpless female.

Since she'd offered to get me development money from the Ontario Arts Council and since, with *Coyote City* a play accompli, I did need the work, I also told her, "But I can make you something."

So I started down the long path that would lead to my second play, a one-act called *The Dreaming Beauty* in which I would meet another ghost, a woman this time.[2]

At first I approached the project rather simplemindedly, thinking I'd just transplant the Sleeping Beauty story to North America.

My first realization was a dramaturgical one, the fact that a play in which the central character lies down and does nothing but sleep would not be exactly exciting no matter what continent or culture it came from.

But then I thought about the importance that dreams have had for me at points of change in my life, about the value our traditional cultures have placed in them, and remembering that there are such things in the dramatic tradition as "dream plays," I knew my work should be concerned with whatever action was going on in the beauty's head as she lay sleeping, with the journey she herself was making.

But then I found a version of the Sleeping Beauty story based on a traditional French text, and it was definitely pre-Disney, a long and rather convoluted adventure about a woman's coming of age in a feudal state. Certainly the prince and love were part of the tale, but so was, for instance, the dilemma of living as a single mother when your husband has gone off to fight a war and nobody in the palace likes you except for your mother-in-law, and she only likes you because she's an ogress and thinks you and the kids look delicious.

It seemed that every woman in the story except the princess had something wrong with her—the fairies were vengeful bitches, the princess's own mother was vain, the ladies-in-waiting were gossips. Each was somehow less than properly a woman, and the story was a blunt message to little girls that the only kind of woman they should grow up to be was the princess.

This, I knew, was not the sort of message I could transplant into Iroquoia unless I was willing to deal with at least being teased for writing the wrong kind of corn.

Part of me also began to worry about more than teasing, about complaints that the media tell us come from radical feminists. "How dare this man," I imagined wan, faceless females screeching, "write a story about a woman's identity!"

But another part of me had already promised a woman I'd do it, and the check from the Arts Council was in the bank, and, well, most of me was just intrigued by the distance between the fictional feudal world of Princess Aurora and my own living matriarchal democracy. Were there any connections? I began playfully making comparisons, contrasts, and decisions.

My first decision was that in a democracy there sure wouldn't be a princess. My central character would have to be a sort of Iroquoian Every Woman, an Indian Any Girl.

And maybe I could replace the fairy godmothers, those guides with gifts, with the Three Sisters, who embody the spirits of corn, beans, and squash.

And I began to suspect that in my play the evil spell that made everyone fall asleep for a hundred years would have to be something like a nightmare five hundred years long, more or less, a bad dream in which—since the Iroquois were an agricultural people—winter never left the land.

Then I knew all at once, or decided suddenly, that my play

had to be another version of post-Columbian history, an allegory from the Six Nations told as simply as any fairy tale, a dream play about the identity of a young woman who was, perhaps, an embodiment of the Iroquoian people themselves.

But this decision seemed to put the love story out of focus and any prince, charm notwithstanding, out of the picture.

It seemed to me that in the world of the Sleeping Beauty, the feudal princess marrying her prince is a story of upward mobility—she gets to move into his castle and family and become a queen. The prince, in the most positive view of the ceremony, in becoming her husband, also magically becomes her lover, her best friend, and her protector (in a less sanguine interpretation, he also becomes her owner).

But I knew that traditional Iroquois culture was more horizontal and that it was the man who had to change residences to marry, who had to move into his wife's mother's or grandmother's longhouse. Neither of their political statuses would necessarily change. I also realized that the man, as a new husband, would of course be her lover and, if it so happened, a friend and the father of her children. But the young woman's oldest brother would retain his roles as her best friend and protector, and the protector of her children. (It seems like a practical arrangement for child rearing in view of the fragility of romantic love.)

I realized then that using those traditional social structures as my guides to the play might be troublesome because it meant that I needed a character to be a brother, not a lover, and that without the required romance a large part of the mainstream audience, maybe even my artistic director, might be disappointed. The play really would be rooted in one of the differences between the cultures.

But I thought about the girl as my own sister then and knew it was right that I write about the girl's brother too.

My artistic director just shrugged away my worries—I don't think she quite understood. "Oh, just be poetic!" she said.

So after most of my women friends assured me that they trusted me to write about this particular female's identity—"Look, Dan, you grew up there. You know who our people are"—the play seemed to just fall onto the page.

Early in *The Dreaming Beauty*, the girl searches for clues to the disappearance of just about everything and everyone she knew in the midst of the never-ending dream of winter. She encounters the ghost.

GIRL: . . . Hello?

GRANDMOTHER: Child, which way's the cornfield? I've lost my direction.

GIRL: Granma?

GRANDMOTHER: There's still a couple of hills to be brought in.

GIRL: . . . Granma, it's me.

GRANDMOTHER: No use leaving them for the crows. Those birds get more than enough to eat.

GIRL: Granma, look at me.

GRANDMOTHER: Big fat black things, just waiting for me to drop my load.

GIRL: Your hands are so cold.

GRANDMOTHER: Did you know I fell down? They got under my feet.

GIRL: Granma, here's my blanket.

GRANDMOTHER: Child, it won't do no good.

GIRL: Granma?

GRANDMOTHER: That's right, child, you remember.

GIRL: Oh Granma.

GRANDMOTHER: Don't be afraid.

GIRL: I'm not.

GRANDMOTHER: Don't feel sorry for me.

GIRL: I love you, Granma.

GRANDMOTHER: That's good. I love you too. But save your love for them who are alive. They need it more than I do.

GIRL: Oh Granma, what's happening?

GRANDMOTHER: I'm happy here, gathering up the last of the corn. I should have it all in before morning.

GIRL: Where's everybody, Granma? Where'd they go?

GRANDMOTHER: You remember that story, child? Your father coming home at dawn, coming up from the river.

GIRL: When I was born.

GRANDMOTHER: That's why he called you Beautiful Daughter of the Dawn. A good name for a child.

GIRL: That's my name?

GRANDMOTHER: Till you grow up.

GIRL: I didn't know.

GRANDMOTHER: Maybe you forgot. It's easy to forget things as you get older. There's so much to remember. So I made this for you.

GIRL: Oh, Granma, it's beautiful.

GRANDMOTHER: The softest deer hide I could make, child. You can keep your medicine inside.

GIRL: I don't have any.

GRANDMOTHER: I know. I was waiting till you grew up to give it to you. But I died first. Stupid birds. But look at this beadwork. The corn design. That's to remind you who I was, how big my house and my fields were.

GIRL: Thank you, Grandmother.

GRANDMOTHER: Promise me you'll grow up sweet and strong like the corn.

GIRL: I'll try, Grandmother.

GRANDMOTHER: Corn silk. Your hair is softer.

GIRL: Granma, wait.

GRANDMOTHER: I have to get back to work.

GIRL: Please stay, Granma.

GRANDMOTHER: It'll all be done by morning.

And the dead grandmother disappears.

My drunken ghost had been one of the lost. Who was this woman?

If the girl is an embodiment of the Iroquoian people, then this ghost of a grandmother with her cornfields and stories and names and bead- and leatherwork seems to be their culture still very alive, the Iroquoian spirit there to guide the beauty back to the land.

It seemed to take the artistic director a long time to get together the money to mount *The Dreaming Beauty*. I imagined, or she may even have told me, that she was struggling to keep her company financially viable. In the meanwhile I entered the play in a contest.

It seemed that whenever I would ask her when the production was likely to occur, she would start muttering about the piece not being quite ready, that she thought I'd not somehow pushed it far enough, that she would give me a call so we could talk about it, a call that never came—because she was too busy raising money, I concluded. Then the play won the contest, and the next thing I knew I'd received an invitation to attend the rehearsals already in progress.

Let's admit that the play had an unfortunate production.

Let's put it down to differences in sensibilities and sensitivities rooted in a shared ignorance of each other's culture.

The young Native actors involved came up to me after the run through and asked me to talk to the artistic director.

Let's just suggest that she didn't quite understand the play.

I remember that the actress playing my good-spirited ghost looked kind of kinky in ballet tights and moccasins, not grand-motherly at all, and that Old Woman Moon, the gentle Grand-mother of All Women, was talking like a banshee. The artistic director said she was just trying to make it magical, ethereal. She wouldn't, couldn't, accept my suggestion that this spirit of light was more down to earth than that, that the play was about getting back in touch with the land.

I remember that my last conversation with the fair-skinned, dark-haired artistic director over the telephone included talk about whether we were having an argument and that I'd wanted to laugh when I heard her saying, "I have a reputation as an artist, you know!"

Maybe I had ended up dealing with the princess after all.

Then one of the actresses injured her ankle, and since there wasn't enough money to recast her parts in the play—maybe all of it was spent on her big plaster cast—she ended up sitting center stage to play all her characters, acting like a human Muppet.

I warned my friends to stay away, had to let my agent deal with the artistic director, and have managed to be civil when I've encountered her at some other play even though for me there's something spooky about her now and her talk of magic and poetry.

Maybe it's simply the absence of a good production of the play that haunts me.

Or maybe I'm sad, finally having understood just how far folks who live in the city can be from people who live on the land.

The last of the ghosts I want to introduce to you is not just another human character who happens to be dead but is instead a rather obviously and intentionally theatrical creature.

I first read a version of the story of Almighty Voice when I was working as a researcher at the Woodland Cultural Center in Brantford, Ontario, probably in the fall of 1978. I knew as soon as I came across the story that someday I would do something with it, write something about it. I made a photocopy and started a file.

Almighty Voice was a young Cree warrior who lived in Saskatchewan near the end of the last century. The spiritual-sounding name is the English translation of Kisse-Manitou-Wayou. His story is usually told by mainstream writers as the story of a sad misunderstanding involving a renegade Indian. In the Cree communities of Saskatchewan, the story still has a life that's almost mythical because Almighty Voice, I know now, became a symbol of resistance.

A short version of the story begins in late October 1895 when Almighty Voice kills a cow. You don't need to know why, or whom it belonged to, if it did indeed belong to anyone. All you need to know is that the Mounties hear about it and arrest him and throw him into the guardhouse.

(The guardhouse still stands as a monument to Almighty Voice in the town of Duck Lake. A nearby building sports a mural two stories tall based on the only photograph we believe we have of Almighty Voice.)

Do the Mounties think they will teach him a lesson? Someone among them perhaps thinks he'll just tease Almighty Voice and tells him that he's going to hang for killing the cow. Almighty Voice escapes and heads off across the prairie.

Is the Saskatchewan River already iced over or does he have to ford, even swim, the freezing river? One of the Mounties decides to go after the Indian, and there certainly is snow on the ground by the time he surprises Almighty Voice a day or so later while he is resting beside a fire.

The details of the encounter shift from version to version of the story.

Let's suppose that the Mountie suggests in English that the young man surrender and that Almighty Voice says in Cree, "Go away! I won't die for no cow!" The result is the death of the Mountie and the start of a manhunt that lasts, off and on, for the next year and a half, with Almighty Voice always just managing to elude the authorities due to his familiarity with the landscape and thanks, no doubt, to his people.

Then in May 1897 Almighty Voice and two of his friends are spotted by a farmer and chased and cornered in a bluff of poplars. All the authorities—Mounties, soldiers, the priest, the Indian Agent—all the settlers, farmers, shopkeepers, traders—all the Indians in the area show up to see the standoff.

Almighty Voice and his friends make like warriors, taunt their enemies, sing their songs. The authorities try to starve them out for as long as it takes for cannons to be brought down from the fort at Prince Albert. They're small cannons, but they work. Almighty Voice and his friends are killed. The End.

When I first read that story, I guess I was innocent, or more accurately ignorant, of the history of that part of Canada. In school I'd been taught that this country had been settled mostly by treaty, and wasn't that civilized and humane?

How unlike the Americans.

I hadn't realized how much space there might be between the lines of such documents, hadn't seen the difficulty in translating between the English and, for instance, Cree languages, between the respective cultures and sets of values, between, for instance, what each community thought was the definition of the word *human*.

When I first read that story, I was shocked by its arc: kill a cow and die. I didn't understand what had gone on; I needed to know more.

I needed to know, for instance, that Almighty Voice was a young man in the first generation after the Riel Rebellion, that the site of the Battle of Batoche was in his territory, and that his was the first generation of people who had been confined on reserves by those nice, humane treaties, the first generation of people for whom buffalo weren't a major source of food and inspiration.

Knowing just these instances, one can begin to understand why a young Cree warrior might kill a cow, how racism started to be institutionalized, why the whites and their government were so scared of one dark-skinned delinquent.

Why he might just spark off another uprising out there in the west!

But when I first started thinking about the story, I hadn't any of these instances in mind. All I had to think about was that dark-skinned delinquent and a situation that seemed the epitome of overkill.

One detail that appeared in a couple of the versions of the story that I came across over the years was the presence of a witness at the killing of the Mountie, a young Cree woman. One version of the story identified her as a cousin of Almighty Voice who was traveling with him as a cook. The other version didn't comment on her role at all, only mentioning in a tone of offended astonishment that after the Mountie was killed, the young woman turned calmly back to tend whatever was cooking on the fire. (How this striking behavior was observed and recorded when no other witness was present was not revealed.)

Maybe it is because I was raised on the Six Nations, where the power of women has always stayed clear, that the presence of the young woman got me to thinking. But wouldn't anyone wonder what that young woman thought she was doing there out in the middle of the winter prairie, away from the village, with that young man and maybe a horse and only the food and weapons they could carry and at least one Mountie following their trail?

The role of cook seemed insufficient reason for her to have placed herself in such peril even if she was a relative. Why couldn't he cook for himself? He was a warrior, wasn't he? The role of wife, however—or even more convincingly, of lover—could make her reasons for being there clear, could make the entire situation seem suddenly more interesting.

I remembered then those black-and-white movies that Hollywood put out after World War II and that I'd seen on television late at night. They presented the sorts of stories in which young lovers get in trouble with authority, and all the idealism their love implies does them no good at all in the face of stupidity and greed and power.

I realized then that what I was looking at was like those *film noir* stories—love against the odds, Bonnie and Clyde, Romeo and Juliet. That sort of love story was more interesting to me than the renegade Indian one that I'd heard all too often before. I could almost see the logo for "A Universal Picture." So I decided I'd write a story about Almighty Voice and that girl, and that my play could be called *Almighty Voice and His Wife*.[3]

I thought it would be fun to find some other version, some

other angle, on those shifting historical facts. I thought it would be both fun and important for my own understanding to find some human explanations for what had happened. I thought maybe I'd even manage to sidestep some of those so-called historical facts.

I guess the one historical fact I was most unhappy with was the bloody ending of the story. Most of me knew I was asking for trouble by choosing to write a story that in fact and by dramatic convention was tragic, but some small and unreasonable part of me just didn't want to deal with the death of Almighty Voice. Even as I came to understand more of the reasons behind that death, it still seemed too stupid, too grotesque an incident either to acknowledge or imagine. And that part of me also just didn't want to be the one to serve up for public consumption yet another image of the defeated wild Indian.

So I thought I could, and plotted that I would, avoid it.

What I intended to do was to stop the story the moment after Almighty Voice and his friends get cornered in the poplars. I thought I could leave them there and so allow at least *my* Almighty Voice to go on living forever, a warrior joyously at war. My concept was for a *coup de theatre* in which I'd set up the audience for a tragic death and then surprise them by forcing their attention away from Almighty Voice and in the direction of all his pursuers.

I wanted to understand what had gone on, and I thought that a good way to do that would be to get into the heads of those people. (Isn't that what mainstream writers tell us the freedom of the imagination is all about?) So I decided I'd create those characters, those Mounties and soldiers and settlers, and that in that way I'd find out just what they as individual human beings thought they were doing to this character I'd started picturing for my own purposes as a sort of Cree James Dean.

It then crossed my mind that if I were going to create all those white characters, then the Native actors I usually worked with would get to play them and that maybe they'd have to wear white-face. The idea amused me.

I felt lucky that some of the early actor training our theatre company had done was in clown.

I must have known, though, that my plan was too abstract to pursue, too didactic and ideological in a naive sort of way, which is to say too preachy and smart-assed. I must also have suspected that in the final analysis I wouldn't be interested enough in those pale-faced characters as individuals actually to create them because as I set out to do my final historical research in preparation for writing, I found myself also turning over in my mind that image of my Native actors in whiteface.

What I found on its other side was the image of white actors in black face.

I looked into the history and conventions of the minstrel show and discovered that troupes performing these entertainments had traveled across much of North America in the 1800s not far behind the settlers. A minstrel show was essentially a variety show peopled by caricatures of stupid but happy blacks on the plantation. The show was performed, of course, by whites.

I knew it was important that minstrel shows had still existed at the time Almighty Voice died. It allowed me to suppose that it would not have been impossible that many of the people who gathered to watch the standoff had also watched and enjoyed a minstrel show, that their attitudes had been partly formed or at least encouraged by the minstrel show's racist stereotypes.

There was a lot about the crudeness and the strictness of the conventions of the language and the characters used in those shows that fascinated and challenged me. Even though I thought the jokes were hackneyed, part of me still found that the ones that mocked our human capacity for stupidity had the bite of truth.

By the spring of 1990 I had a pile of research and all these ideas, and not one scene on paper. But I was ready and I got lucky. I was accepted into the Playwright's Colony at the Centre for the Arts in Banff, Alberta. As I rode the bus from the Calgary airport through the foothills and into the mountains, the first images of the play came into my mind.

A projected title: "Act One: Running with the Moon"

Then another projected title: "Scene One: Her Vision"

A drum heartbeats in night's blue darkness. The full moon sweeps down from the sky like a spotlight to show and surround White Girl asleep, fetal on the ground. The drum begins a sneak-up beat, the moon a similar pulse. White Girl wakes at the quake, gets to her feet, and takes a step. The drum hesitates. A gunshot and a slanting bolt of light stop White Girl, blocking her path, blocking out the moon. Three more shots and slanting bolts of light come in quick succession, confining her in a spectral tipi. She peers out through its skin of light at Almighty Voice, a silhouette against the moon. He collapses to the beats of the drum, echoes of the gunshots. White Girl falls to her knees as the tipi fades and the moon bleeds.

So my first act did tell the entire tragic story as a poetic but straightforward narrative. I couldn't resist the conventions of the tragedy or the love story, both of which seem to require supplies of tears. I did manage to find at least a lyric moment of victory for my warrior in the birth of a son at the end of his year-and-a-half run, just before he goes bravely to his death.

I'd also found this young woman with the evocative name of White Girl, who it seemed had been one of the first from her community ever to be taken away to an industrial—residential—school to be nearly Christianized. I also knew that she'd had to go on living after Almighty Voice had died while the rest of the settling of the West occurred.

And I'd done it all with two actors.

My second act, entitled "Ghost Dance," happened as a vision of my own, probably on the stage of the auditorium of an abandoned industrial school in Duck Lake.

Both of the actors are now in whiteface, the man who played Almighty Voice in act one is now the Ghost of Almighty Voice, the woman who played White Girl now plays the Interlocutor, who is a white man, and the master of ceremonies of something that seems like the ruins of a minstrel show. The Interlocutor also looks a lot like the Mountie that Almighty Voice killed in act one and seems concerned only with getting the Ghost to toe the line in the Red and White Victoria Regina Spirit Revival Show.

The act re-examines the story of act one through the non-narrative conventions of the minstrel show: songs, jokes, satire, and dance. The clear drama of the act begins as the Ghost realizes that White Girl still exists inside the character of the Interlocutor. The Ghost then starts to take over the show, to use its conventions to reawaken and remind White Girl about herself.

(Following the minstrel show convention, scenes are announced through the use of title placards on a tripod.)

Daniel David Moses

The Interlocutor, fleeing the Ghost, bumps into the placard stand. "SCENE EIGHT: STANDUP" turns up.

GHOST: Sir!

INTERLOCUTOR: Did you know, Mister Ghost, that marriage is an institution?

GHOST: Yes, sir, I had heard that said.

INTERLOCUTOR: Well, sir, so is an insane asylum! Did you know, Mister Ghost, that love makes the world go round? Well, sir, so does a sock in the jaw! Which reminds me, sir. An Indian from Batoche came up to me the other day and said he hadn't had a bite in days. So I bit him! Do you know, sir, how many Indians it takes to screw in a light bulb?

GHOST: What's a light bulb?

INTERLOCUTOR: Good one, Mister Ghost, a very good one. Well then, sir, if it's nighttime here, it must be winter in Regina. Nothing could be finah than Regina in the wintah, sir. Am I making myself clear? Does this bear repeating? Does this buffalo repeating? Almighty Gas, you say! Answer me, Mister Ghost. Answer! What! A fine time to demand a medium! It's very small of you, sir. I promise you I will large this in your face if you do not choose to co-operate. Tell me, is it true that the Indian brave will marry his wife's sister so he doesn't have to break in a new mother-in-law? Does it therefore follow, sir, that our good and great Queen Victoria keeps her Prince Albert in a can? That's where she keeps the Indians! Hear ye, hear ye! Don't knock off her bonnet and stick her in her royal rump with a sword, sir. The word, sir, is treason. Or are you drunk? Besotted! Be seated, sir. No! Stand up! You, sir, you, I recognize you now. You're that redskin! You're that wagon burner! That feather head, Chief Bullshit. No, Chief Shitting Bull! Oh, no, no. Blood thirsty savage. Yes, you're primitive, uncivilized, a cantankerous cannibal! Unruly redman, you lack human intelligence! Stupidly stoic, sick, demented, foaming at the maws! Weirdly mad and dangerous, alcoholic, diseased, dirty, filthy, stinking, ill-fated degenerate race, vanishing, lazy, mortifying, fierce, fierce and crazy, crazy, shit, shit, shit, shit . . .

GHOST: What's a light bulb?

INTERLOCUTOR: Who are you? Who the hell are you?

GHOST: I'm a dead Indian. I eat crow instead of buffalo.

INTERLOCUTOR: That's good. That's very good.

The lights shift from variety to spectral as the spotlight finds the placard: "SCENE NINE: FINALE."

INTERLOCUTOR: Who am I? Do you know?

GHOST: I recognized you by your eyes.

INTERLOCUTOR: Who am I?

GHOST: White Girl, my White Girl.

INTERLOCUTOR: Who? Who's that?

GHOST: My fierce, crazy little girl. My wife. Ni-wikimakan (my wife). . . .

The Ghost goes and dances in celebration to a drum. The woman removes the white . . . face and costume, becoming White Girl again. She gathers the costume in her arms as the spotlight drifts away to become a full moon in the night. White Girl lifts a baby-sized bundle to the audience as the Ghost continues to dance in the fading lights.

My guess is that *Almighty Voice and His Wife* works like a purging or an exorcism, that the Ghost spooks the Interlocutor and the audience. It feels like it gets a lot of the poison out.

A more recent play seems to have ghosts only in its title and in the minds of the characters. It doesn't go breaking through fourth walls or other conventions.

What it does do is explore the source of the poison.

The three white people in *The Moon and Dead Indians,* the first play of two in *The Indian Medicine Shows,* gather around a cabin in some foothills in New Mexico in 1878, barely living on the land, survivors of the frontier who are haunted by a denial of their part in that process.[4]

JON: Your hands are like ice. I'll go build up the fire.

MA: I heard them, Jonny.

JON: What?

MA: That's why I was afraid.

JON: Let's not talk about it, Ma.

MA: But I heard them.

JON: You didn't.

MA: Coming across the valley. You know the way sound carries. They were down in the pine bush.

JON: They wouldn't make no noise.

MA: Their horses do. They can't make their horses be sneaky.

JON: Ma, look at me.

MA: The hooves on the rocks as they crossed the brook. Knock-knock. Knock-knock. Even I could hear it.

JON: There ain't no Indians.

MA: I could hear the leather of their saddles creaking.

JON: They's all gone. All the redskins vanished.

MA: It's the sound of death coming, Jonny. You know that. You know the sound of death.

JON: Ma. Ma, look at me.

MA: What is it?

JON: They's all rounded up, Ma. Rounded up or shot.

MA: What's wrong, baby?

JON: There's no Apaches round here no more. You know that. No Apaches, no Comanches, no more God–damned wild Indians!

MA (slaps him): Don't talk to me that way!

JON: Jesus protects us, Ma.

When I was first writing *The Moon and Dead Indians* for a twenty-four-hour playwriting contest during Nakai Theatre's Whitehorse Writers Festival, what happens in the play appalled me. A glib description of the crime might use the words *sex, violence,* and *racism.* I couldn't believe it was coming out of me. I kept trying to comfort myself, explained the bad behavior of the characters, the final horror of the piece, by saying with some irony that it had to be because this was my first play with white characters.

But I really don't see the world like a politician.

A friend, Wayson Choy, recently published his first novel, *The Jade Peony,* and in reading it I was reminded that the Chinese community, too, used to, maybe still do, refer to white people by words that translate as *ghosts.*

And certainly the anguished characters of *The Moon and Dead Indians* are lost, souls far from their homeland, their people.

Would that fair-skinned, dark-haired young man who turned away hurt and angry from the drunken ghost in *Coyote City* understand these characters any better? Would my artistic director?

White as a color exists only because some of us get told that we're black or yellow or Indians. I think my ghosts exist to probe this white problem, this tonal confusion, to spook its metaphors. Maybe my ghosts are like mirrors but from a fun house.

I want to spin new meanings out of the stereotype or turn it into a cliché in trying. Once white itself is a ghost, color will be just a too simple beginning of rich and strange complexities.

We'll all have tender skins.

Strange I am, I guess, being interested all along in the palefaces and why they seem to want everyone to be as lost as they are. But it happens after a while. You end up related to some of them, and you don't want your own people going off alone.

Yes, it's curious fun.

But someday Native actors will get to play the parts in *The Moon and Dead Indians,* and unlike me, they won't even imagine needing to do it in whiteface.

VOICE OF THE LAND

 GIVING THE GOOD WORD

Elizabeth Woody

As an *Indian* from the Pacific Northwest, I have a relationship with a place and a community whose origin extends back through a multimillennial span. Belief in this origin is very important to my community. Yet because of a limited perception held by a large number of non-Indians, this belief does not garner respect for my community as the first people.

At the beginning of contact between Northwest Native cultures and non-native newcomers, much was exchanged to benefit trade relations. Newcomers benefited from Indian knowledge of land, plants, and animals. With the exception of diseases and addictions, the start of relationships in that time period was cautiously beneficial. Distortion of this relationship due to a lack of information exchange about origins and a lack of personal respect between people, however, disrupted power sharing. Subsequently, this has affected personal growth, tribal governance, and tribal-state relationships down to today.

To respond to that disruption, we must become aware of how our society's good points, particularly in the Northwest, come from many perspectives woven together through time. Not long ago, Warm Springs tribes in Oregon expressed concern about the need to preserve pioneer grave sites along our reservation borders. In the *Portland Oregonian,* Delbert Frank, then the Warm Springs tribal chairman, was quoted as saying that the graves deserved respect and protection because of our joint history. This is complicated. I was awestruck; I had never thought of our past being tied together. However, recognizing one's ignorance establishes a pattern or structure that can generate a form of knowledge. Knowledge comes from personal work and investment, and to "grow knowledge," we set a trellis as a form for the climbing vine.

We are born, we live, we die. This is grossly simplistic, yet it is all I know of my ancestors. When I look at my genealogical charts and government census files, I am saddened. This may be all I will ever know about my ancestors.

I am prevented from knowing more. No documents recorded their stories. I have to imagine their story. Often through handmade objects of my ancestors, I sense from their choices and responses to materials used in these articles that my interpretation of history is limited. It becomes altered in the transfer of possession, in the sense that objects that once belonged to us were collected and separated from their communities of origin. On seeing these artifacts, a psychological moment is triggered: these objects served a greater purpose than beauty and function, and in my attempt to honor their memory I must see their makers in terms of ancestral celebration and intelligence.

My heritage, political history, and family narratives are mixed with the recent experiences of cultural genocide and disruption. Contact by Indian people with the Lewis and Clark Expedition had a great and immediate impact on American society, and through trade and excursions many indigenous people came to know about eastern events. But there was very little meaningful contact between the expedition and the tribes. In fact, it was irritating to Meriwether Lewis that the presence of newcomers—his expedition—wasn't considered more important by the busy Columbia River Indian people. The result of that expedition, however, was to have a great and irreversible impact on my people in the next century and beyond.

The coming of the white man was predicted by visionary Dreamers, who were indigenous healers and prophets able to "see" with extreme clarity, and it was talked about for a long time in the years of adjustment and negotiation that followed. The discussions did not say that we were dealing with a certain type of people but rather with a destiny that could not be avoided. It was not idle or fearful talk, and I imagine the discussions were similar to ones I hear today: that we are necessary to this land and we must endure along with our beliefs and spiritual and cultural practices.

Many tribes in the Pacific Northwest went from prosperity and independence to landlessness and dependency. Modoc and Paiute people, for example, as well as many western Oregon tribes, suffered removals during the land rush by homesteaders who wanted the prime lands of Oregon Territory. Then there were the wars fueled by political unrest in the region and fears of possible uprisings generated by newspapers and the government. The Wounded Knee Massacre and the removals of Plains Indian people were reflected in the Northwest in the brutal treatment of indigenous people by vigilantes and the military.

One's identity as an indigenous person—an Indian—is a hard and difficult awareness when you look at Indian extermination and removal, much of which was subsidized by the U.S. government for the purpose of westward expansion. And when you really look, you soon realize that this happened in order to ensure that non-Indian newcomers would take root in a way that meant that enormous amounts of people, forests, and animals in this rich homeland would be dispossessed or destroyed.

My identity is best asserted and understood when I begin by saying I am an enrolled member of the Confederated Tribes of the Reservation at Warm Springs, Oregon. I have an identity card that lists my indigenous lineage of Navajo, Yakama, Wasco, Warm Springs, and Pit River Indian people. In more detail, I am a descendant of the Wishram, Wasco, Watlala (usually known as Cascade), and Pit River tribes on my maternal grandfather's side. On my maternal grandmother's side, I am Tygh and Wyampum. From my father, I am Diné and born for the Tódích'íi'nii.

As you can see from my maternal lineage, many bands and tribal units have intermingled from both sides of the Columbia River system and its tributaries. I am also aware of a mixture of English (probably Welsh) and possibly Hawaiian and Spanish ancestry, although I haven't found documentation for this conclusion. The mixture pleases me, yet I cannot claim a voice within those ethnic literatures, communities, and cultures. Like most U.S. citizens, I have a tenuous connection to several perspectives and land bases.

My Indian tribal enrollment is possible because I was born to a people who are the progeny of the first citizens of this continent. As a descendant of the first citizens, who possess a prior and inextinguishable legal claim to the land, I'm also aware of how we Indian people continue to be members of a colonially instigated, reservation-based system of government. This government is nevertheless sovereign, as in my tribe's case at Warm Springs, and it looks to tradition for an assertion of reserved rights, law, and identity. Through my tribal membership, I know that federal recognition of our political units, presently called tribes, began with the signing of the Treaty of 1855 at Walla Walla, Washington.

This treaty, which affirms federal recognition of Indian tribal sovereignty, preceded Oregon's statehood by four years. With the uneasy backdrop of history between Oregon tribes and the state of Oregon, former governor Barbara Roberts once commented as an offhand joke that she had been reminded by a tribal official that the state government is a *junior* government. While the relationship between Oregon and its Indian tribes is not discussed in every community venue, this relationship is important to understand and maintain for all people. For instance, the current crises in resource management in the region are being resolved in part by collaboration on several levels between these respective governments.

Warm Springs tribes and others in Oregon are diverse, complex entities. We maintain an intangible connection to the land, people, and culture that is described and known as the Voice of the Land. This connection is part of a process known in our belief system as an original instruction from the Creator. Today, tribal policies are determined and managed by the religious and cultural shape of the issues at hand. For example, contemporary tribal governments now determine policies and future requirements for membership in the tribes. As an outcome of this, I am eligible to enroll in one or another tribe but only if I choose one of them. For instance, I can enroll in the Confederated Tribes and Bands of the Yakama Nation, or I can enroll in the Navajo Nation. But I will remain enrolled at Warm Springs because for five generations my maternal ancestry has been part of the people there.

Standards have been set by contemporary tribal governments that may fracture this lineage in the future. If descendants are ineligible for enrollment because of the fragmentation of blood quantum, who will receive the reserved rights of our sovereign status? I am 16/32 Navajo—which means my father was a full-blooded Navajo—12/32 Warm Springs, 3/32 other tribes, and 1/32 European descent. My mother is Wasco of Warm Springs, Wasco of Yakama, Watlala of Yakama, Warms Springs, and 1/16 other. This may not make much sense to many people, but Indian membership rolls can be as complicated as any other registry.

This can be disorienting when talking about enrollment status and eligibility, which concern living individuals. Since I am not a full-blood by current blood quantum laws, if I have children they will not be eligible for enrollment in the Northwest tribes of which I am a descendant. If it is decided that I am ineligible for services and benefits because I choose to live and work off the reservation, I will accept that status as well as I can. Because circumstances like these are being discussed on my home reservation, tribal enrollment requirements should be examined.

As tribal peoples, we have valuable water rights, natural resource reserves, and rights to learn about and maintain subsistence lifeways, including the spiritual consideration of our home country. Salmon, edible roots, berries, deer, and elk, and revered predators like bear, cougar, wolf, coyote, eagle, hawk, and owl are major partners in this lifeway. To ensure the survival and integrity of long-established relationships with the aforementioned beings and to promote the abundance and affluence of all beings, Gail Tremblay, a Native American writing colleague from the Northeast, has said, "When we speak of resource management, it is our way of talking in a common language."

These connections and relationships aren't made evident through talk alone but in the daily enjoyment of animals and the environment around us. On seeing animals and plants wherever they are, whatever their behavior, people I know and respect express pleasure about their companionship and coexistence. Once, watching chickadees at a fast-food business, my mother said, "Those birds look so pitiful being beggar birds. Look at them eat french fries. No wonder they are so scraggly." About the flocks of noisy crows in what we call the Conference Tree near her house in Portland, my aunt has commented, "No manners. All talking at once, not listening to others. They only like to hear themselves talk." One may think that my mother and my aunt were humanizing these birds, but they were commenting on how our human behavior and their bird behavior are alike. The adaptation in the birds' lifestyles is in response to their environment. We shape their world as they shape ours.

One spawning season, my uncle took me to a small creek that had been restored to a "natural" condition by the Natural Resource Department at Warm Springs. Heavy equipment had brought boulders and logs to provide shade and hiding places for returning salmon. He made me walk quietly up the creek bank until we saw a salmon doe waiting for her mate to appear. He told me salmon bucks would soon arrive and fight for a place beside her. She would wait as long as she needed to. If there was a fight, the contest would not be long because "There is not much time to waste" in this season, and the loser would continue to look for an available mate.

When it was time, the salmon would dance on their tails in the sand for the spawning redds. She would put eggs in the depression, and he would provide the milt. Whether they mated or not, they would die. They would die alone or together. If the buck didn't make it up the creek, there would not be a spawning dance. "Whew, now isn't that a love story," my uncle said. I smiled and agreed.

A community is made strong by individuals who accept responsibility for themselves. Example is a good method for teaching responsibility. It creates genuine community within families, since a community can exist and determine its future only when people are free to be individuals within the framework of family. Before you become a participating individual, you need to work through family dynamics to understand how you were made and why your family is what it is. We also choose secondary families through friendships and alliances. I have seen times, however, when a decision to be true to oneself has worked against my particular family. In the 1950s, for example, my grandparents, Lewis Pitt Sr. and Elizabeth Thompson Pitt, made their choice to move fourteen miles off the reservation to Madras, Oregon, for personal reasons of independence.

My support system has been primarily my family and secondarily the tribes. The tribes have provided for most of my higher education, since scholarships are endowed by the revenue from our corporations. I have used the benefits of being, in essence, a shareholder in the many businesses the tribes maintain. These shares provided me the necessary time to establish myself as a writer and artist, especially in my college years, when I had to gamble that my tenacity would help me in a difficult field. My past employment as a professor at the Institute of American Indian Arts, as well as my involvement in the literary community of the Pacific Northwest, was made possible because of these benefits. I have also been an independent contractor, giving readings and workshops, serving on panels and task forces, working as a studio assistant and, later, studio manager for my aunt, Lillian Pitt, who does ceramic art. In observing my aunt at her studio, I have learned firsthand the challenges of running a business while maintaining creative integrity in one's work.

My mother, Charlotte Agnes Pitt, gave me a place to stay and the use of her old Royal typewriter when I returned from the Institute of American Indian Arts. She loaned me money and provided me transportation locally to give performances. She also fed me and watched my home when I left on long trips. My family has helped me in innumerable ways. Lewis Pitt Jr., my uncle, spent long hours of discussion with me during my childhood and adolescence. He answered many questions I was grappling with in my life and in my poetry. Later, I read that in the older Indian traditions of the Chewana/Columbia River Plateau, a maternal uncle was responsible for the intellectual training of his sister's children.

There were many ways for families to interact and maintain strength. In addition to my family, my close friends were always there to help me in whatever way they could. I am indebted to all of them. Being a responsible adult does not happen only because of your gifts or desires but because of your continual personal investment and sense of gratitude toward people who have helped you to develop yourself. This success benefits the whole. Hard work is not a chore but an investment and the result of the collaboration of many people.

As it is applied by Indian tribes, blood quantum is not an indicator of tribal continuity, nor does it measure the extent or degree of continuity. Yet it has affected my past and will affect my future because of the nature of tribal policies. It is a very sensitive issue for me. Often I reflect upon the story told by my grandfather, Lewis Pitt Sr., about his life. I know how he was shaped by loss and why he believed in family love and solidarity. The breakdown of his family in a difficult period of tribal history impacted greatly upon his sense of security. He lost his parents and siblings at a very young age, and he lost his family inheritance and a ranching livelihood.

In earlier years, his grandparents and parents had made the

transition fairly well from fishing and working as artisans and tradespeople to ranching. They became educated and wealthy. Perhaps they were regarded as threatening because of that—threatening, at least, to those who would rather see Indian people kept in ignorance and poverty during the transition period of their removal from ancestral lands to less valuable reservation lands.

As a teenager, I met an elderly man at a yard sale who asked if I knew a Lewis Pitt. I said I was his granddaughter. He told me that as a child he had grown up and played with him. They were children of two big ranches in the area which were, so to speak, sister ranches. The ranchers combined their ranch hands and resources and worked together in rounding up cattle, branding, and gathering hay. He said he was very fond of Lewis's family—they were very good people. The man gave me a load of silk neckties I was admiring, and he gave me a look of admiration that was an uncommon experience for me with a non-Indian man in Jefferson County. I wish now I had been mature enough to stay and ask him more questions about that time.

Lewis Pitt Sr. and his younger brother, George Pitt II, had parents who were from both sides of the Chewana/Columbia River. Lewis was enrolled in Yakama, and George was initially enrolled in Warm Springs but changed his enrollment to Yakama later in his life. They lost their family in childhood, and, as orphans, they were sent to distant relatives and a boarding school. Their father died as a result of bad surgery in 1924, and my grandfather said his mother, Charlotte Edwards Pitt, died not long after of a broken heart. Her death was not due exclusively to grief but also in part because of her treatment by the power structure then in place in Warm Springs.

Charlotte was technically an outsider because she was a Yakama tribal member even though she came to live on the Warm Springs reservation with relatives when her parents died. She spent her early years on the reservation with her younger brother and sister, Harrison and Edith. When it was time for her to marry, she chose to delay her marriage to George Pitt I until her siblings were old enough to take care of themselves. The estate of George Pitt I was eventually divided among Charlotte's two remaining sons and a third person, a girl named Gertrude Bagley. In the estate proceedings, the mother of Gertrude Bagley put forth her child's claim to be recognized as an illegitimate heir.

As a dowager, Charlotte Pitt had little authority in the management of the estate, and because the American system did not bestow much freedom upon women during that era, she was subjected to cruel treatment by the court. I have to remember she was vulnerable at that time. From descriptions of Wasco-Wishram-Watlala women in traditional society, I believe that Charlotte was inclined to be a strong and proactive individual. The matter of paternity was settled by testimony based on speculation about George I's whereabouts and relationship with Gertrude's mother at the approximate time of conception. I feel a sadness for Charlotte and Gertrude in this matter, and it is an event that hurt my grandfather and his brother. It is also an event that, for several generations, my family has found difficult to address.

The separate tribal membership enrollment of Lewis and George Pitt II was the wish of their mother, who was of Wasco-Wishram-Watlala descent. This was because of her marriage to a Wasco man from the Oregon side of tribal groups that spoke a similar language and that had a similar culture. There was a lot of intermarriage between different tribal groups, including the Yakamas, Umatillas, Walla Wallas, and so on. Bonds were formed this way for centuries. We are very conscious of this in terms of our need to transcend tribal boundaries in order to collaborate on joint projects and discuss issues of mutual importance.

Much of the lands held across state and Indian reservation borders were held in individual allotments initially divided among living members of the tribes at the time of allotment. These lands have been reabsorbed into the tribally owned land base or lost to non-Indians through legal land sales. The federal government's allotment system promoted individual land ownership and sale to individuals within the new boundaries. These lands were taxed if they were original allotments, and they were available for sale to outside people.

My grandparents viewed the land allotments they inherited and owned as heirlooms, and they regarded them like the presence of a relative who had passed away. Many of my family's allotments have been reabsorbed into the tribal land base. Current federal laws prohibit the sale of allotments to outsiders and forbid outsiders to be inheritors of allotments. This makes it difficult for offspring of intertribal marriages to inherit land. My grandparents were unaware of these newer laws. They held on to their land for their children, and we learned of these laws only after my grandfather's death. Much of the land that once belonged to my grandparents is no longer in our possession. While it is acceptable to me that the Yakama Tribes possess these lands, blood quantum has worked against my family.

It is important for me to say that we were given compensation for the land and the old-growth timber. On federal or trust land, however, natural resources and their material worth are not appraised by the government at fair market value but rather at a *much lower rate*. Deals struck with independent companies and corporations via government contracts enable the independent contractors to buy raw materials at a small fraction of their worth. Such was the case with our estate at Yakama. It is a hard exchange. It was because of this inequity, along with the current inheritance laws, that my family rejected the offer the Yakamas made at the time of grandfather's probate and initiated a court challenge concerning the appraised value of the land.

The litigation has erased all record of Lewis Pitt Sr.'s enrollment in Yakama. I wrote the Yakama tribal enrollment office for his genealogical chart and received a document concerning someone from the Wannassay family. In the legal systems brought from England, property and land ownership constitute a strong legal position, but possession does not have a strong position in Indian systems of property and land ownership. Our family had to appeal and pursue our claim through a separate federal legal system for land claims and inheritance while opposing the Yakamas, which was a situation we were not prepared for, since we consider ourselves Yakama too.

Official tribal chronicles have numerous gaps in them. For example, there are stories about my great-grandparents holding meetings at their ranch to translate news from the English language into the Indian language for people in Warm Springs and to discuss the news. There are also stories of times when people from other reservations across the state came to my grandparents' home in "Hollywood" to discuss the formation of a tribal constitution and by-laws. My grandfather was secretary-treasurer during the formation and adoption of the Warm Springs Tribal Constitution and By-Laws, which were ratified on February 14, 1938, but he is not listed on official plaques in the Warm Springs Museum.

In a similar oversight, George II, my great-uncle, is not listed on the tribal college graduates roster. I recall my grandparents saying they lived in a tent during the early years of their marriage to help him through his studies at the University of Washington.

A remarkable quality of character, existing apart from official records, is shown in the vitality of the people who participated in hours of heart-filled discussions. My aunt Lillian says, "They would passionately discuss politics while we kids played. People would go to sleep when tired, wherever they could find a place. Others would pull out their instruments and play music and sing for hours. Then stories would be told. It was an amazing time."

These individuals participated in an older system of government, social structure, and affiliation with one another. The ancient trade network that preceded the separation of people into reservations was a communal method of associating and discussing ideas. There are stories of mysterious events occurring, of brilliant people having "accidents." I can see how warnings like "Sit down! Be quiet! Don't stand out!" became the norm. My aunt has cautioned me, "It is alright to use family stories to inform your work, but you will need to have the strength to back it up." My mother's comment on my writing was: "Remember, your capacity to heal is through your words. We need to hear them too."

Census files from 1855 onward at the Oregon Historical Society show that several people with our family name disappeared. In some instances, dates of death are noted. But in some cases, whole family units become absent from the files. It is easy for me to imagine that these people made their decision to make their way as free citizens and left the Warm Springs reservation. This reinforces my belief that I can exercise my individual right to choose where I will live, how I will work, and whom I will marry. I do not see how it is wrong for me to do these things as a tribal member.

To exercise the precious benefits of my tribal enrollment, I can still participate in the tribal system in meaningful ways. I will still be a member of my family. I will still be able to contribute in some way to the people I come from. I will also learn about my father's Navajo side of the family and feel pride and loyalty to his people. But I feel isolated, too, from both sides of my family as I make my way as a writer and artist. This may come from too much self-examination. Writing takes time. Once a friend tried to coax me into going to a distant powwow with her by saying, "Why read and write about Indians when you could just be one for a while?"

When I discussed with my uncle Lewis Pitt Jr. the possibility that our Indian children will not be eligible for enrollment in the Confederated Tribes at Warm Springs, he said that the current trend indicates that being "a full-blood Warm Springs" is the ideal. To ensure that our blood remained pure, we would immediately have to chart family genealogies and plan marriages between us. Most concerns center on the limitations of our land base. There is not much land to share among so many. I understand that, but it goes against my belief that we are a generous people.

To maintain a nation of eligible tribal members, it seems one cannot marry in perpetuity only for love. Like our treaty rights, we cannot pass on our citizenship without documentation. Perhaps some can argue that "romantic love" was brought about by a Western mind-set, yet I still believe love is a powerful force that molds one's life and mind. This belief was set for me when I heard my great-grandparents' and grandparents' stories about their courtships.

My great-grandfather and great-grandmother wrote to one another at the turn of the century. As I stated before, she was in Yakama, and he was in Warm Springs. Through letters he proposed marriage to her, and she wrote back that she would marry him if he was willing to wait. She was the oldest of three children, and because they were orphans, she was raising the younger two. George waited. She eventually wrote for him to come get her, and he packed horses with supplies and began his journey to Yakama. At that time, crossing the Chewana/Columbia River meant he had to swim across holding on to his horse's tail.

The Catholic and Presbyterian Churches had divided up the territory in order to get converts to their faiths. George was Presbyterian, and Charlotte was Catholic. After Charlotte had herself absolved from the Catholic Church, the two were married in Stevenson, Washington. Then, the story goes, they swam across the great river holding on to their horses' tails, and they honeymooned on their journey back to Warm Springs. An old trunk in the garage held their letters. When our house burned down in 1973, no one thought to see if the letters were salvageable. Now that old trunk and their letters are only memories, like their courtship.

My grandmother told a story about seeing my grandfather as a young man walking down the road with a group of men. They were workers in the Civilian Conservation Corps, and she was working for a government employee. She said she had savings and her own car. Although her relatives pressed her about marriage, she was not so inclined at that time. She had employment, and she was also a practitioner of the traditional religion, which was very time-consuming. Men wanted her in the married way, but she did not get sidetracked—that is, until she saw my grandfather walking down the road laughing and joking with other men. "That's him! Who is he? I would like to go out with him," she said.

My grandfather had never kissed a woman until he kissed my grandmother. She said, "I had to ask him out, pick him up in my car. I even had to kiss him first!" He was the boy from the Pitt Ranch who had a deer named Blossom that danced with matching palominos in the Fourth of July parade. I am guessing, but I think that really got to my grandmother because she loved deer.

She told me this story one day when I, as a young woman, went to see her. My grandmother also said, "Go to school. Take care of yourself first. You don't have to get married. If you do and you love him, you will know why." This is something my grandfather told me also. This may not seem traditional; maybe it isn't. And I don't even know if it is romantic. It seems you have no choice except to listen and follow your own internal voice.

My grandmother went to the Presbyterian Church with my grandfather. She made the decision to be a church member with him, and he likewise participated in certain ways with her family. I recall taking my grandmother to "doings," the Shaker Church, and her family's ceremonies. Both of their funerals were held in the Longhouse and the church.

Controlling knowledge of the past is an indoctrination process, and as I see it, it is definitely separate from the spiritual tradition of my family. Personal history is present-minded, and it is an innovative and consistent method for looking at one's life. For personal and social health, balanced action, and peace, it is important to see how our lives are shared and affect all things. Land is not exclusive property but is the embodiment of our ancestors. The concept that all beings have a purpose has allusions to spiritual stories and to the term *time immemorial,* which is a sense of time difficult to comprehend.

What is time immemorial? Is it the time preceding written time, which is the time after the Treaty of 1855? Is it the time of 14,000 years of continuous habitation at Celilo Falls (Wyam), or the 14,500 years of living in the Columbia River Plateau? I believe it is more than the total of these epochs combined. My grand-parents insisted we have been here since the beginning of human-ity. This was the time Coyote first appeared after Creation to make way for our presence.

The Declaration of Sovereignty drafted by Warm Springs tribes in 1991 contained the term *Ne-shy-chus*. In the Sahaptin lan-guage this phrase declares that the indigenous or Native cultures of the Columbia River Plateau possess an innate sovereign prerogative and that we are rooted in an ancestral domain that preceded the Treaty of 1855. Before the treaty, we were free of outside influences. The treaty was made with a fledgling U.S. government, an entity that was considered tenuous. The tribes signed the treaty to pro-mote peaceful compromise and coexistence between the original inhabitants and the newcomers seeking land. It was an agreement of "good word," and, I feel, it was made so that the relationship between the original people and the newcomers would flourish.

We are free to follow our indigenous cultural practices and religion. "Congressional plenary power does not preempt natural laws of the Creator," Walter Spedis of Yakama stated simply. Our cultural practices are simple and straightforward; societal structure is flexible, allowing for ways of maintaining sovereignty; tribal po-litical units with shared principles follow similar practices during cultural events and spiritual observances. This is the characteristic nature of Columbia River Plateau societies, which are empowered by what Warm Springs people characterize in the saying "Tee-cha-meengsh-mee sin-wit ad-wa-ta-man-wit," which means, "At the time of Creation, the Creator placed us on this land and gave us the voice of this land, and that is our law." This unwritten law has been practiced in accordance with instruction handed down from one generation to the next in song and ceremony. In communal observances, this instruction, spoken in the Indian language, is meant to sustain a seasonal renewal of the environment, and its essence brings strength and integrity.

It is a primary practice of a "mentality of abundance," which is based on the idea that there is plenty on earth for everyone, which is brought about by good thought and a response from the divine. Flourishing occurs by the active power of individual and communal thought in prayer. The "good word" is a connection to a greater intelligence that unifies us. Through personal and collective observance, thought affects the seasonal migration of the salmon and the return of natural plant foods. There is abundance continuously without a fragmented resource management system based on profit, private control, and bureaucratic institutions.

The present-day decline of the salmon is more than an economic crisis in the Northwest. We Indian people have failed to regenerate our thought for the sake of the salmon, especially by not teaching all who live in the Northwest the necessity of abiding by the natural laws of a complex ecosystem. In the few generations since 1855, 14 million salmon and steelhead have dwindled to 2.5 million, and an even more dramatic decline is presently occurring. The new "Nor'wester" is threatened and suffering as we are also, along with our plant and animal relatives on this land once abundant, as we experience a life characterized by scarcity and extinction.

The Chewana/Columbia River has been broken up by twenty hydroelectric dams, most of them built without concern for the cyclical life pattern of the migratory salmon. This is further exacerbated by nuclear, agricultural, and industrial pollution, as well as the evaporation of water from reservoirs and the clear-cutting of forests. All of these intensive activities muddy, warm, spoil, and deplete the watershed in land areas both green and arid.

Drought is a cyclical concern in the Northwest because of

the El Niño current and the massive loss of evergreen forests, which are being cut down at an even faster rate than tropical rain forests. A transpiration process brings rain to the region because of trees "calling and giving to the rain." Snowmelt water from the snowpack of the Cascade Mountains filters through forest soil. Without this transpiration there is little or no rainfall, and we now have a limited water supply. An overall environmental/economic crisis in the Pacific Northwest has resulted in the polarization of societies, cultures, and people, and the "voice of the land" has fragmented into matters of hard cash and a loss of jobs.

The dispossessed and unemployed cannot seek retribution for the destruction of an ecosystem. Integrity is not a viable argument for change in industry, because when old resources are exhausted, industry simply moves on to cheaper resources in other parts of the world. In a free-market economy, citizens do not have a right to have jobs or a guarantee of a quality of life that depends on heritage or an ancient ecosystem. Because it takes centuries, we cannot expect to regenerate entire forests in our lifetimes. What is important for people to comprehend is that the Indian tribes mentioned herein possess a valid document and an inalienable right to honor and protect their heritage and the ancient ecosystem of which they are a part. In squabbles over a fair market and a fair share, we must support Indian tribes in their efforts to ensure that life will continue.

The practice of traditional awareness in a simple and direct way, taught from time immemorial, is to take only what is needed and to let the rest grow. The basic law of genetic development regarding biodiversity is proliferation. The idea that form follows function is basic to science. Current timber industry plans for fifty-year harvests as "sustainable yields" will only ensure sterile tree farms. At clear-cut sites there is little hope for the regrowth of primal soil- and life-rich forest environments. When there is little left to function, there will be less. Salmon are a major component of this since their spawning provides bodies that nourish trees that shade, cool, and purify spawning grounds.

Three-hundred- to five-hundred-year-old trees do not need to be cut down. When only 5 percent of the forest land as of 1994 was ancient forest and 30 percent of that has been designated for harvesting, a return to ancient principles and practices is imperative. National Public Radio broadcast a report that trees are bought and submerged into the ocean as *savings*! This is done by those who can purchase the timber to ensure against future exhaustion and take advantage of scarcity, from which they will realize tremendous profits! Living trees are priceless on any terms, and they are devalued by cutting them in this manner.

An awareness of cultural continuity and worldwide interconnected intelligence is necessary. We need to examine what Warm Springs tribes have learned from the integration of heritage, political savvy, and family initiatives. This knowledge is the source of what I know and appreciate about the courage of the people I have observed and learned from in my lifetime. Despite intrusions, disruptions, anger, and numb sorrow, I still feel the holy aspects of the land. Because it draws upon ancestral power and a belief in healing, this knowledge is nurturing. The need for personal and social health is not exclusive to the Americas or to my Indian relatives alone; it is a necessity we share in common.

"The voice of the land" gave Indian tribes at Warm Springs a way to be an integral and beneficial component of the land. We must see how we all share responsibility for the land, and we must realize the detrimental impact of global colonization. People outside of indigenous cultures are now experiencing the negative effects of history, especially regarding overall health conditions in the Americas. We all feel the consequences of apathy, guilt, addictions, alienation, and self-loathing. In order to heal, we must free ourselves from the selfish practices of acquiring and hoarding wealth.

Community health is not easily attainable, however. Warm Springs tribal leaders have decided we need to be an optimally healthy community by the year 2000. To become healthy, we need an understanding of genetic needs and instruction in how to care for our bodies. During the Sunday Washat/Worship services at the 1992 Pi-Ume-Sha Pow Wow, a soft-spoken woman said, "Our lives are made stronger by purity. Our teachings have been telling us for a long time what we need to do. We are getting sick from eating foods that have not been treated well or with respect. We drink water that has things in it, things that shouldn't be there. If you eat foods the Creator gave us, you are bringing strength to your body, to your children, to your people."

An awareness of one's physical being must involve a desire for optimum health combined with a desire for a better community. My maternal grandparents' stories of childhood, with their bleak details of being orphaned and suffering the loss of family, were small events in the shadow of larger grief. But their words and actions showed me that their faith and trust were what contributed to their survival. In hearing their story, I also heard of their inextinguishable desire to stay alive and develop the ability to create the foundation or form for their family to grow upon. My grandparents' story is not uncommon. Each one of us has survived. This land in the Pacific Northwest is where we arose, and where we thrive, and where we grow, and *this is my trellis*.

A few years ago, I was walking with my aunt Lillian in downtown Portland while a protest was being staged by loggers and their families. Signs saying "I Like My Spotted Owl Fried" and logging paraphernalia were brandished. With all sincerity, my aunt said, "Those poor people. They are like the Indian fishermen, and they don't even know why this is happening to them." Later, after I told my uncle Lewis about this, he said, "We are all in this together, except we, as tribal people, will not leave or neglect our responsibility to the land. We don't have that luxury. There is too much at stake."

Many Indian leaders come from an informed and wise lineage. From the center of themselves they believe in the "good word" and in the idea that all beings originated from the same source. They believe we are a phenomenal motion of connected intelligence. My grandmother and Andrew David, her first cousin, spoke of this power as life moving through each of us for a certain purpose or task given to us. This means we should respect others for their gifts and should acknowledge and value their presence. The need to expand cultural knowledge is the need to help others access this life force. Even in our most helpless state, we must work for the resolution of our problems. As Indian people, we are neither exotic cultures nor symbols of atrocity and injustice. We are the acknowledgment that what destroys life is part of us and that we are inextricably involved with those who oppose us.

At a repatriation meeting with the U.S. Army Corps of Engineers, Delvis Heath, Warm Springs chief, stated, "In the way we operate, the word given is to be honored. It seems that in this day and age, agreements are put on paper. Once done, the word is forgotten. If you lose this paper next week, it's as if the word never existed." Through the practice of traditional knowledge, we thank the earth, the life force of the sun, and the Creator; and we bring the earth into our lives by knowing its life. The land, the human individual, and the seen and unseen are connected through the "good word" to the bonds of love's teaching, healing, and strength.

My grandmother took the time to teach me. Her work continues. My grandfather fished in the traditional manner. His son continues to work for the possibility in the future. By reclaiming possession of our native Indian selves, we are within the authentic sources of our heritage. On my Wasco side, I am a direct descendant of Bear, Salmon, and Cougar. On my Diné side, I am born for one of the clans brought into this world from the being of Spider Woman. My relatives remain devoted. They sing, pray, and heal.

Te Waka Toi: Contemporary Maori Art, an exhibit at the Burke Museum in Seattle, Washington, was closed by Maori elders with a ceremony. Indigenous people from the Puget Sound area came to help with the closure. The first Puget Sound tribal group walked us through the display, stopping at each piece with a song. They said, "Our ancestors were here and asked us who these people were. We explained through song and blessed and cleansed each piece." The next Puget Sound tribal group took us through again in a similar manner. They released the ancestors who wanted to be released.

Vi Hilbert, an Upper Skagit elder and storyteller, spoke to the Maori people in the Salish language, which is exquisite to hear. The ceremony hummed with incredible sensitivity for the soul of the art and its makers. It was a long event, and when the Maori elders finally gave their closing, they said, "We are not copying anyone here. It seems we are much alike in our ways. We are of one earth and mind. It makes us happy to experience this." They began to sing, and a young man with tattoo markings and wearing a flax skirt led the way. With his club poised and his face holding intense expressions, his stances were dramatic and distinctive as he shouted and stomped at each art piece. We walked with the Maori people, just as they had done, respectfully following previous songs with the Puget Sound people.

Ceremonies like these, and our memories of them, will continue. They cannot be revoked or exterminated. The corruption of our indigenous image and identity does not represent our real and varied lives. Imitations of surface elements arising from our combined histories, which superimpose themselves on our authentic and real cultures, are invalid, and they are not enough. Made strong by temperance, we—as Indian people in heritage, identity, and outlook—know our own self-worth. And we, who are irreplaceable carriers of our own story, know that self-worth does not come from the measurement of ancestry through blood—it comes from ourselves, our work, and our story.

LAND SPEAKING

Jeannette C. Armstrong

I want to discuss the intensity of my experience as an Okanagan who is indigenous to the land I live on and how that experience permeates my writing. It is my conviction that Okanagan, my original language, the language of my people, constitutes the most significant influence on my writing in English. I will discuss how my own experience of the land sources and arises in my poetry and prose and how the Okanagan language shapes that connection.

I want to comment on the underlying basis for how this occurs within my personal experience of the land as an Okanagan-speaking writer. I will emphasize the significance that original Native languages and their connection to our lands have in compelling the reinvention of the enemy's language for our perspectives as indigenous writers.

As I understand it from my Okanagan ancestors, language was given to us by the land we live within. The land that is the Okanagan is part of the Great Columbia River Basin on the interior plateau of Washington State and British Columbia. The Okanagan language, called N'silxchn by us, is one of the Salishan languages. My ancestors say that N'silxchn is formed out of an older language, some words of which are still retained in our origin stories. I have heard elders explain that the language changed as we moved and spread over the land through time. My own father told me that it was the land that changed the language because there is special knowledge in each different place. All my elders say that it is land that holds all knowledge of life and death and is a constant teacher. It is said in Okanagan that the land constantly speaks. It is constantly communicating. Not to learn its language is to die. We survived and thrived by listening intently to its teachings—to its language—and then inventing human words to retell its stories to our succeeding generations. It is the land that speaks N'silxchn through the generations of our ancestors to us. It is N'silxchn, the old land/mother spirit of the Okanagan People, which surrounds me in its primal wordless state.

It is this N'silxchn which embraces me and permeates my experience of the Okanagan land and is a constant voice within me that yearns for human speech. I am claimed and owned by this land, this Okanagan. Voices that move within as my experience of existence do not awaken as words. Instead they move within as the colors, patterns, and movements of a beautiful, kind Okanagan landscape. They are the Grandmother voices which speak. The poem "Grandmothers" was written in N'silxchn and interpreted into English. The English term *grandmother* as a human experience is closest in meaning to the term *Tmixw* in Okanagan, meaning something like loving-ancestor-land-spirit.

GRANDMOTHERS

In the part of me that was always there
grandmothers
are speaking to me
the grandmothers in whose voices
I nestle
and draw nourishment from
voices speaking to me
in early morning light

glinting off water
speaking to me in fragile green
pushing upward
groping sun and warmth
pulling earth's breath
down and in
to join with porous stone
speaking to me
out of thick forest
in majestic rises to sheer
blue
in the straight slight mist
in twigs and fur
skin and blood
moon and movement
feathers stroking elegant curves against wind
silent unseen bits
in the torrent of blood
washing bone and flesh
earth's pieces
the joining of winds
to rock
igniting white fire
lighting dark places
and rousing the sleeping moment
caught in pollen
a waking of stars
inside
and when blue fire
slants to touch this water
I lift my eyes

and know I am seed
and shooting green
and words
in this hollow
I am
night glittering
the wind and silence
I am vastness stretching to the sun
I am this moment
earth mind
I can be nothing else
the joining of breath to sand
by water and fire
the mother body
and yet
I am small
a mote of dust
hardly here
unbearably without anything
to hold me
but the voices
of grandmothers[1]

The language spoken by the land, which is interpreted by the Okanagan into words, carries parts of its ongoing reality. The land as language surrounds us completely, just like the physical reality of it surrounds us. Within that vast speaking, both externally and internally, we as human beings are an inextricable part—though a minute part—of the land language.

In this sense, all indigenous peoples' languages are generated by a precise geography and arise from it. Over time and many generations of their people, it is their distinctive interaction with a precise geography which forms the way indigenous language is shaped and subsequently how the world is viewed, approached, and expressed verbally by its speakers.

I have felt within my own experience of travel to other lands of Salishan-speaking people an internal resonance of familiar language and familiar land. I can hear the N'silxchn parts in all Salishan languages. I have been surprised by how unfamiliar sounds in those languages resemble and resonate closely with the physical differences between their land and mine. The language lets me feel the points where our past was one and lets me "recognize" teaching sites of our common ancestry. The poem "Ochre Lines" imitates the way N'silxchn engages a constant layering of land and human experience within its imagery.

OCHRE LINES

skins
drums
liquid beat fluttering under the breast
coursing long journeys
through blue
lifelines
joining body to body
primeval maps
drawn under
the
hide
deep
floating dreams past
history
surging forward

upward
through indigo passages
to move on the earth
to filigree into fantastic
gropings over the land
journeys marking
red trails
a slow
moving earth vision[2]

I experience land as a fluent speaker of Okanagan. N'silxchn, the Okanagan land language, is my first language, my Earth Mother language. When I close my eyes and my thoughts travel, N'silxchn recreates the sounds, the smells, the colors, the taste and texture precisely. N'silxchn emulates the land and the sky in its unique flow around me. I feel its vast outer edges touching the sky and the horizon in all that I experience as life. I feel it speaking the oldness of earth, speaking to us. I have given English voice to this sense of N'silxchn land presence in my grandmother landscape poems. The poem "Winds," from that series, intertwines land presence through my human voice presence.

WINDS

Winds	moving			clouds
past		earth		sky
are		one		moves
around	me	silent		colors
drifting	sometimes	present		dark
with	soft		white	
			flakes	touching
life		rich	lacework	unknown
	hands		twined	with care

Jeannette C. Armstrong

a place	forever	still	tracing	quietly
a line	stretched	to a	horizon	
fading			with time	and gently
ending		breath[3]		

As it is spoken today, the Okanagan language carries meanings about a time that is no more. Its words speak of a world different in experience from this one. Its words whisper more than the retelling of the world. Through my language I understand I am being spoken to, I'm not the one speaking. The words are coming from many tongues and mouths of Okanagan people and the land around them. I am a listener to the language's stories, and when my words form I am merely retelling the same stories in different patterns. I have known this about my language since learning English as a second language. Learning English as a second language allowed me to "hear" the different stories in English words from those that N'silxchn brings forward from its origins. I now know this is true of any language. I hear words speak old stories. The poem "Words" emerged through an exercise in both languages to capture N'silxchn imagery interpretive of such an illusive and abstract concept as meaning.

WORDS

Words are memory
a window in the present
a coming to terms with meaning
history made into now
a surge in reclaiming
the enormity of the past
a piece in the collective experience of time
a sleep in which I try to awaken
the whispered echoes of voices

resting in each word
moving back into dark blue
voices of continuance
countless sound shapings which roll thunderous
over millions of tongues
to reach me
alive with meaning
a fertile ground
from which generations spring
out of the landscape of grandmother
the sharing
in what we select
to remember
the physical power in thought
carried inside silently
pushing forward in each breathing
meaning wished onto tongues transforming with each
    utterance
the stuff of our lives
to travel on wind
on air
to bump wetly
against countless tiny drums
to become sound
spasms coursing upward into imagine
there to turn gray silence
into explosions of color
calling up the real
the physical
the excruciating sweetness of mouth on mouth
the feltness of the things of us

then settling soundless
colorless
into memory
to be hidden there
reaching ever forward into distances unknown
always linking to others
up to the last drum
vibrating into vast silence[4]

By speaking my Okanagan language, I have come to under-stand that whenever I speak, I step into vastness and move within it through a vocabulary of time and of memory. I move through the vastness into a new linking of time to the moment I speak. To speak is to create more than words, more than sounds retelling the world; it is to realize the potential for transformation of the world. To the Okanagan, speaking is a sacred act in that words contain spirit, a power waiting to become activated and become physical. Words do so upon being spoken and create cause and effect in human interaction. What we speak determines our interactions. Realization of the power in speaking is in the realization that words can change the future and in the realization that we each have that power. I am the word carrier, and I shape-change the world. The poem "Threads of Old Memory" was an inquiry in English-language imagery of the N'silxchn concept of speaking as a pro-found and sacred responsibility.

THREADS OF OLD MEMORY

Speaking to newcomers in their language is dangerous
for when I speak
history is a dreamer
empowering thought
from which I awaken the imaginings of the past

bringing the sweep and surge of meaning
coming from a place
rooted in the memory of loss
experienced in ceremonies
wrenched from the minds of a people
whose language spoke only harmony
through a language
meant to overpower
to overtake
in skillfully crafted words
moving towards surrender
leaving in its swirling wake
only those songs hidden
cherished
protected
the secret singing of which
I glimpse through bewildered eyes
an old lost world
of astounding beauty

When I speak
I attempt to bring together
with my hands
gossamer thin threads of old memory
thoughts from the underpinnings of understanding
words steeped in age
slim
barely visible strands of harmony
stretching across the chaos brought into this world
through words
shaped as sounds in air

meaning made physical
changers of the world
carriers into this place of things
from a place of magic
the underside of knowing
the origination place
a pure place
silent
wordless
from where thoughts I choose
silently transform into words
I speak and
powerfully become actions
becomes memory is someone
I become different memories to different people
different stories in the retelling of my place
I am the dreamer
the choice maker
the word speaker
I speak in a language of words formed of the actions of the
    past
words that become the sharing
the collective knowing
the links that become a people
the dreaming that becomes a history
the calling forth of voices
the sending forward of memory
I am the weaver of memory thread
twining past to future
I am the artist
the storyteller

the singer
from the known and familiar
pushing out into darkness
dreaming splinters together
the coming to knowing

When I speak
I sing a song called up through ages
of carefully crafted rhythm
of a purpose close to the wordless
in a coming to this world from the cold and hungry spaces
    in the heart
through the desolate and lost places of the mind
to this stark and windswept mountain top
I search for sacred words
spoken serenely in the gaps between memory
the lost places of history
pieces mislaid
forgotten or stolen
muffled by violence
splintered by evil
when languages collide in mid-air
when past and present explode in chaos
and the imaginings of the past
rip into the dreams of the future

When I speak
I choose the words gently
asking the whys
dangerous words
in the language of the newcomers

words releasing unspeakable grief
for all that is lost
dispelling lies in the retelling
I choose threads of truth
that in its telling cannot be hidden
and brings forward
old words that heal
moving to a place
where a new song begins
a new ceremony
through medicine eyes I glimpse a world
that cannot be stolen or lost
only shared
shaped by new words
joining precisely to form old patterns
a song of stars
glittering against an endless silence[5]

The Okanagan language, as I have come to understand it from my comparative examination with the English language, differs in significant ways from English. Linguists may differ from my opinion, arguing that the mechanics of grammar differ but the functional basis of the two languages does not. I will not argue. I will only say that I speak Okanagan and English fluently, and in so doing I perceive differences that have great influence on my worldview, my philosophy, my creative process, and subsequently my writing.

Okanagan is completely vocally rooted in that it has never been written down. It is a language devised solely for use by the human voice and the human body. The elements inherent in that are straightforward. A good example is the N'silxchn method of differentiating between the word for 'this', *axa* (used only with something you can touch), and 'that', *ixi* (used only with something near, as in a room) and 'that over there', *yaxis* (used for something farther away but still only when you can point at it), the last with a voice stretching of the vowels to indicate far away. In a vocally rooted language, sound, with all its emotive qualities, determines how words are used and forms a backdrop in meaning, as do gesture, stance, and facial expression.

While this seems to impose limitations on what one has available for descriptive imagery in written languages, actually the opposite occurs. The range is broadened by the way the sounds in words can be combined and the way each sound can be used, in much the same way that classical music stretches the imagination by the various mathematically possible ways sound elements can be combined.

Over time, the Okanagan language has acquired a music-based sensitivity in the creation of meaning. The sound elements of tempo, beat, rhythm, volume, and pitch have a greater significance for comprehension than in languages that rely on visually based imagery. The language re-sounds patterns of action and movement as imagery. This is what the Okanagan people mean when they say that everything is a singing. Sounds solicit emotion even in babies; certain sounds cause sadness, and certain rhythms cause excitement. Sounds "speak" in particular ways of inner response. Music relies on such responses to communicate its message. In the same way, Okanagan, as a vocally based language, relies heavily on sounds and sound patterns to communicate meanings.

N'silxchn recreates sounds of the land in its utterance, but it also draws on the natural human emotional response to sound and rhythm to contain and express a philosophical or spiritual idea. The poem "Frogs Singing" is the result of a long discussion on our language and worldview with my sister Delphine, who spoke only Okanagan until age twelve. She pointed out that the stars and the frogs in the Okanagan summer nights have the same rhythm and that in saying it to recall the sound and the night filled with stars, the rhythm filled her soul and became hers.

FROGS SINGING

my sister did not dream this
she found this out when she walked
outside and looked up and star
rhythms sang to her pointing their spines of light
down into her and filled her body with star song
and all around her
frogs joined the star singing
they learned it
long ago[6]

It has become apparent to me that, for the most part, English lacks this kind of musical coherence. For the most part, the "sounds" of the words and the rhythms created in their structure clearly are not constructed to draw a musical response. In fact, the language is deaf to music and only chances on it through the diligent work of writers. Perhaps this has to do with the loss of the body as the sole carrier of words. Perhaps literacy—with its marks on stone, wood, paper, and now in electronic impulses—silences the music that writers are able to retrieve.

Okanagan is a language guided by active components of reality. Syllables form base units that carry meaning in the language. Root syllables are where meanings reside rather than only in whole or complete words. Words are a combination of syllables, each of which carries meaning and contains function. Each word, when examined, can be broken down into root syllables, each of which has an active meaning and when combined activates a larger animated image.

An example is the Okanagan word for dog: *kekwep*. The word has two syllables. The first syllable, *kek,* is an action syllable meaning something like "happening upon a small (thing)," and the second syllable, *wep,* meaning something like "sprouting profusely (as in fur)." In English, the two together would not make specific sense. However, when these two syllables are combined in Okanagan, they immediately join together to become an activator of a larger image. They create an action together—fur growing on a little living thing—made familiar only by a connective experience.

When you say the Okanagan word for dog, you don't "see" a dog image, you summon an experience of a little furred life, the exactness of which is known only by its interaction with you or something. Each such little furred life is then significant in its own unique way. Although each dog bears the commonality of having fur and being little and particularly familiar, no kekwep can ever be just a dog.

Speaking the Okanagan word for dog as "an experience" is quite different semantically from reading the English word *dog*. The English word solicits an inanimate generic symbol for all dogs, independent of action and isolated from everything else, as though a dog without context and without anything to which it is connected could really exist. It must be a frightful experience to be a dog in English.

In Okanagan, then, language is a constant replay of tiny selected pieces of movement and action that solicit a larger active movement somehow connected to you by the context you arrange for it. Times, places, and things are all made into movement, surrounding you and connected to you like the waves of a liquid stretching outward. The following excerpt from my novel *Slash* gives an example of this sense of time and place merging into one through imagery in my prose.

> She came and knelt in front of me. She took my hands and spoke my Okanagan name softly. I had a strange feeling like I did when I heard the dance songs inside my head. I felt like I was made of mist or something and I melted into the scene around me. She said in our language, "We are now more than one. We have become three. Your son will be born in the springtime when the saskatoon flowers bloom. He will be named to your side of the family."
>
> I couldn't speak. All I could do was reach out and pull her to me and rock her while the feeling washed over us. I knew she felt it. Somewhere in my head, I saw us from another point of view, just a little above us, like through clear glass. I saw us kneeling and moving with the rhythm that flowed around us in shimmering waves, then we grew smaller and smaller until we were just a speck on top of that mountain and our land was vast and spread out around us, like a multicolored star quilt.[7]

In the Okanagan language, perception of the way reality occurs is very different from that solicited by the English language. Reality is very much like a story: it is easily changeable and transformative with each speaker. Reality in that way becomes very potent with animation and life. It is experienced as an always malleable reality within which you are like an attendant at a vast symphony surrounding you, a symphony in which, at times, you are the conductor.

Fluent speakers of both English and indigenous languages

sometimes experience a separation of the two realities. I have experienced this separation, and it has fascinated me since my formative years as a learning storyteller and later as an interpreter for my elders at ceremonial and political gatherings. My concern as a writer has been to find or construct bridges between the two realities.

In the use of English words, I attempt to construct a similar sense of movement and rhythm through sound patterns. I listen to sounds that words make in English and try to find the sounds that will move the image making, whether in poetry or prose, closer to the Okanagan reality. I try, as in the example below, to create the fluid movement of sounds together with images in a fashion that to me resembles closely the sounds of the Okanagan.

> Tonight, I sit up here at the Flint Rock and look down to the thousands of lights spread out in the distance where the town is creeping incessantly up the hillsides.
>
> Across the Okanagan valley the sun begins to set. Blazes of mars-red tinged with deep purple and crimson brush silvery clouds and touch the mountain tops. The wind moans through the swaying pines as coyotes shrill their songs to each other the gathering dusk. Long, yellow grasses bend and whip their blades across cactus, sand and sage.[8]

In North American colloquial English, I have found some of the rhythms I search for. I find them more abundant in Rez English, so I often use Rez English in the prose I write, as in this example from "This Is a Story":

> Actually Kyoti himself was getting pretty sick and gaunt from eating stuff that didn't taste or look like

food. Especially real food like fresh salmon. But the headman would just shake his head and say, "Get out of here, Kyoti. Your kind of talk is just bullshit. If you say them things, people will get riled up and they might start to raise hell. They might even try to do something stupid like break the dams."[9]

Okanagan Rez English has a structural quality syntactically and semantically closer to the way the Okanagan language is arranged. I believe that Rez English from any part of the country, if examined, will display the sound and syntax patterns of the indigenous language of that area and subsequently the sounds that the landscape speaks. I believe it will also display, through its altered syntax, semantic differences reflecting the view of reality embedded in the culture.

An example is the Rez English semantic pattern that subverts and alters the rigid sequential time sense compelled by the way the English language grammatically isolates verb tense. Standard English structures a sentence like this: Trevor walked often to the spring to think and to be alone. Rez English would be more comfortable with a structure like this: Trevor's always walking to the spring for thinking and being alone. The Rez style creates a semantic difference that allows for a fluid movement between past, present, and future.

Another example is the way spoken Rez English often seeks to supplant a divisive disposition in human interaction revealed in English grammar through the designation of gender-based pronouns. Mother-tongue speakers of Okanagan experience great difficulty in the use of the gender-based pronouns. They most often seek to leave them out. An example of spoken Rez English that seeks a balance would be structured something like this: Mary was talking with Tommy about the balky car and then the talking was on how to fix it. In English this would be: Mary spoke to Tommy about the balky car, and then she talked with him about how it could be fixed.

In Okanagan storytelling, the ability to move the audience back and forth between the present reality and the story reality relies heavily on the fluidity of time sense that the language offers. In particular, stories that are used for teaching must be inclusive of the past, present, and future, as well as the current or contemporary moment and the story reality, without losing context and coherence while maintaining the drama. There must be no doubt that the story is about the present and the future and the past, and that the story was going on for a long time and is going on continuously, and that the words are only mirror-imaging it having happened and while it is happening.

I concern myself with how to capture and express that fluidity in my writing. I have found a serious lack of fluidity in English grammatical structure. Perhaps here may be found the root of the phenomenon that gives rise to the discussion about linear and nonlinear reality.

My writing in English is a continuous battle against the rigidity in English, and I revel in the discoveries I make in constructing new ways to circumvent such invasive imperialism upon my tongue.

THE STONES WILL SPEAK AGAIN

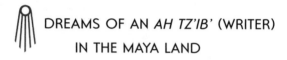 DREAMS OF AN *AH TZ'IB'* (WRITER)
IN THE MAYA LAND

Victor D. Montejo

The Dream

There are many circumstances that can push someone to write or to become a writer.[1] In my case, as a Mayan in a small community in the Kuchumatan highlands of western Guatemala, the desire to write was really a dream. Since most Guatemalan Mayans are illiterate, their exposure to reading and writing is minimal. In consequence, the ability to write was considered something special, a gift from which Mayans were excluded. At least this was the belief among Mayans and non-Mayans when I grew up. Now, living in the United States, I can see in retrospect, as an adult, those days when I grew up as a boy in the highlands of Guatemala.

During the early 1950s there were very few schools in the Mayan villages of this region, and it was hard to dream of having a professional career, or even studying, for that matter. If the children were asked what they were going to be when they grew up, everyone would answer *campesinos,* or corn planters, as were their parents. To achieve any level of education, even to reach the sixth grade in school, was very difficult because there were no schools, and teachers did not want to work in these isolated places.

This was the situation for Mayan people in the western highlands of Guatemala until the Maryknoll missionaries arrived in this region during the early 1960s. In my town, Jacaltenango, in northwestern Guatemala, they built a hospital and started a boarding school for Mayan children. This is where I began my formal education.

I remember how harsh the teachers were that the Maryknoll nuns hired. To avoid punishment in the first grade, for example, I had to memorize my reading assignments. This was and still is the way Mayan children are forced to read and write in Spanish. In the boarding school, we had a library where we could read tales from fantasyland if we wanted, but most children preferred to listen to the stories the elders or their parents told, because we believed those events occurred in our own homeland and were not foreign. We could relate to the stories, and they helped us to maintain our identity as Mayan children.

When I finished primary school, I got a scholarship to study for three years in a seminary far away from my homeland. This was the San José Seminary in Sololá, Guatemala, a very good school directed by the priests of the Benedictine Order. As an adolescent, I became interested in reading books about the missionaries' adventures in faraway places, such as Africa, Asia, and South America. I then started to wish I too could write books, although sometimes I thought a person should travel all over the world in order to have the ideas needed to write books.

This was a difficult time for the Mayans. Mayan culture was seen as deteriorating, and the Natives were disrespectfully called *indios*. I questioned myself about the validity of my own Mayan culture. Was it good enough as a source for writing? Should a Mayan even dream of writing? These were my internal conflicts while I read books for pleasure. But whenever I returned to the village where I grew up, I again listened to Mayan stories and other tales from the people around me.

I remember that it was during this time that my mother told me a terrifying story about my grandfather who died and came back to life again. My grandfather was kidnapped by a spirit and taken forcibly to the underworld. My mother said that he refused to serve as an *alkal txah* (prayer maker), a sacred office among the Mayans. It is believed that if a person refused this service to God and the community, the person could become ill or have an accident and die suddenly. He was shown the various punishments given to the souls that have committed crimes and major sins while living on earth. When I read the *Divine Comedy*, by Dante Alighieri, I started to think about its similarities to the dream, vision, and experience of my grandfather. I thought there were fascinating things to be told about the Mayans.

In 1969, I received a scholarship to go to the Instituto Indígena Santiago in Antigua, Guatemala. The institute was a boarding school for young Mayan men who were pursuing careers as primary-school teachers. The discipline at the institute was very severe, and I did not have permission to leave the old monastery that served as a school or the chance to socialize with other young people beyond the restricted environment of the institute. Perhaps my lack of a romantic life pushed me into more reading, especially since I studied world literature in one of my classes.

At this time, too, I started to have many incredible dreams. I well remember a dream in which I saw myself walking up a hill with friends until we finally reached the top. The top of the hill was flat and was planted with corn ready to be harvested. Suddenly I saw myself alone, standing on a chair in the middle of the cornfield. On a table in front of me there were three books, and in my hands I had another, which I was showing to the people, though no one was there; only the corn plants were standing around me. I was surprised to see the titles of the books, which I can't remember now. But on the covers of the books I could read the name of the author: Victor Montejo.

I awoke very intrigued by the dream, so I started to ask myself, Can it be possible that I, Victor Montejo, would write books in the future? I continued to think of that dream all the time, to remind myself of a possible mission for me to accomplish for my people. For Mayans, dreams are important as windows through which to gaze into the future.

I continued to study, but in the meantime I also started to write down the dream of my grandfather. On one occasion I asked my mother to tell the story again. She was a little bit afraid to tell it. Life beyond the physical one has to be treated or reflected upon with care and respect. Those souls who inhabit it are not like us anymore. But she told me the story again, and I started to write it out by hand. I did not have a typewriter, so I had to write fast in order not to make my mother uncomfortable while she told me the story. She had memorized the story a long time ago and told it whenever she was asked to. While I was writing the story, some passages scared me. It was as if I were actually seeing or experiencing what grandfather had told the people about that near-death experience after he awoke some forty years before.

When I had finished writing down the 200-page story, I bought my first typewriter and carefully typed it. After the manuscript, which I titled "Cries in the Darkness," was finished, I took it to one of my teachers, Brother Sebastián, who read it and suggested, "This is good stuff, but you should get rid of those sections where you included beliefs of Hinduism. Remember you are a good Christian." That comment surprised me since I did not know anything about Hinduism, nor did my mother. She had told me the story in our Popb'al-Ti' Mayan language, and I had written it in Spanish.

Following my teacher's suggestions, I dropped some sections and took the manuscript to him again. He liked the story and told me to have it published. I was incredibly happy, and I accompanied him to a press in Ciudad Vieja, near Antigua Guatemala. The publisher liked the story, but then the publisher told me that since I was not yet a known writer, I would need to pay 200 quetzales in order for him to print 500 copies of the book. I did not have the money at that time.[2] My parents were poor campesinos; I was able to attend school only because of scholarships. As a young man trying to write, I felt helpless and frustrated, so I took the manuscript home and forgot about it completely. I began to think that writers must have a lot of money to be able to have their books published.

When I finished my training to be a primary-school teacher, I was offered a teaching position, and I went back to teach in my own community. The environment of the village schools was depressing. The adobe buildings constructed by the villagers had small windows, dirt floors, no libraries, and no educational material for teaching the children. Teachers had to buy their own textbooks and reading materials if they wanted to improve their teaching techniques.

There was a lack of didactic material from Western sources. I realized that Mayan culture was very rich, but unfortunately no Mayans were writing for their own people. I began to think about my Mayan heritage and decided to write stories and legends that were fading from the oral tradition. It was necessary to document the oral histories of the Mayan people in order to secure a place for ourselves in the modern world, which was strongly assimilating younger generations of Mayans. Although I already had the bad experience of not finding a publisher for my work, I insisted on writing for the sake of preserving and promoting the Mayan culture. This is how I wrote *El Q'anil: The Man of Lightning,* which was published in the United States in a bilingual edition in 1982 and 1984.[3]

In Guatemala, Native values are not supported officially but are instead being eliminated. To be an educated Mayan and a writer during the late 1970s and early 1980s was very dangerous. In an effort to bring an awareness of our situation and to promote our culture, a group of schoolteachers founded a newspaper called *Despertar Maya* in 1978. It soon died because we did not have financial support for it and because the majority of the people in this region did not have the habit of reading. Many of the people simply did not know how to read. I was also advised anonymously that the newspaper should be closed or we would be "in trouble."

An Appreciation of the Ancestors' Way

This, then, was my beginning as a writer. A genuine appreciation for my Mayan culture and my desire to make it visible to the outside world made me write down the stories and legends of the Jakaltek people. It was not the desire to become a popular writer which moved me to write; it was my desire to speak and leave a written legacy for new generations to come. I continued to remind myself constantly of my dream in the cornfield, and I continued to write. I am convinced that we modern Mayans, like our ancestors, have a lot to tell the world, and we need to find ways to express our creativity even under difficult circumstances.

I am aware of the difficulties Native people have in writing our stories. In the past, the Ah Tz'ib' Maya wrote magnificent texts carved on stones and monuments in their Classic Mayan language. Following that tradition during early colonial times, the Ah Tz'ib' Maya wrote their histories in Mayan languages but with Latin characters. Those writers were compelled to write their accounts because their traditional ways of life were fading away as a result of colonial domination. Mayan culture and the ways of the ancestors were assimilated, changed, or eliminated, but Mayan written tradition continued through ethnohistorical sources very well known today among Mayans, namely the *Popol Vuh,* the *Chilam Balam,* the *Annals of the Kaqchikeles,* and the *Título de Totonicapán,* among others.

Through these sources we recognize two major trends in Mayan literature. First, the documents serve historical purposes concerning land claims, because they reaffirm the Mayan presence and ownership of the land they occupy. Second, the same ethnohistorical documents provide stories and legends that give Mayan culture its historical roots and antiquity. In other words, the ethnohistorical documents mentioned above serve to document Mayan history and our right to the land, and to express Mayan creativity through the spoken and written word.

Unfortunately, and because of the position of powerlessness in which Mayans have been kept by the ruling non-Maya elite, we have been replicating the work and repeating the complaints of our ancestors. It is hard for Mayans to be creative when we are constantly struggling for our very survival in the violent environment of Guatemala and of Chiapas in Mexico. Because of this struggle, I myself have tried to write both culturally and politically since, in the case of Mayans, the two approaches are strongly interrelated.

From a cultural standpoint, I am proud of my Mayan culture and I want to make my culture known in all its greatness. Much knowledge is being forgotten because there is no real recognition that each Mayan language is a carrier of knowledge and wisdom through oral tradition. In some cases, Mayans talk about the greatness of their ancestors as non-Mayans do but do not show that this ancestral culture is still providing exceptional knowledge and values for the present. It is thus necessary constantly to create or recreate Mayan culture in order to revitalize it and make it live for the future.

Politically, it is not possible to remain silent in the face of the repression that has affected our culture. The great Mayan tradition is still vital today, but it cannot express itself freely because of the policies of assimilation and expropriation that encroach on our lives. Thus I consider that the role of the modern Mayan Ah Tz'ib' is twofold: to express the greatness of Mayan culture through his or her creative writing, and to denounce the atrocities committed against our people.

This is the strategy that I have followed in my writings. In my book *The Bird Who Cleans the World and Other Mayan Fables,* I emphasize the creativity of modern Mayans, while in *Testimony: Death of a Guatemalan Village,* I wrote as an eyewitness to one of the massacres committed against Mayans of northwestern Guatemala during the early 1980s.[4] I consider it a moral responsibility of the Native writer to be a voice for the people and to let the world know about not only the achievements of his or her people but also the crimes committed against them. I believe that the Native writer has much to do on issues of human rights, especially in this time when the indigenous people of the world are making their presence felt more strongly than ever.

The Modern Mayans and Their Cultural Struggles

My more recent writings concern issues of human rights, Mayan ethnicity, and nationalism. There is now a pan-Mayan movement of ethnic reaffirmation, and this too has its own history. For example, during the 1960s and 1970s, most Mayans were not happy to be Indians. If young people managed to move to the city for higher education, they stayed there for work and did not return to their communities. The term *indio* had a profoundly negative connotation for them. More recently, the indigenous people of Guatemala have been discussing and reaffirming their identity as Mayans.

For example, several organizations now use the name *Mayan*. The most important of these Mayan organizations are the Consejo de Pueblos Mayas de Guatemala (COM-G) and the Council of Mayan People of Guatemala (COPMAGUA). The latter is an umbrella organization that coordinates other Mayan organizations that deal with the political and cultural struggles of the indigenous people in their negotiations for peace in Guatemala. Another organization is the Academia de las Lenguas Mayas de Guatemala (ALMG). The ALMG is of major importance because it is the first autonomous institution directed by Mayans to promote the Mayan languages and cultures. The ALMG includes Mayans from the twenty-two different Mayan linguistic communities in Guatemala. In other words, it is the first officially recognized organization that has a nationwide presence. This institution supports projects of ethnographic research and literature that are promoting writing and a knowledge of Mayan culture among the Mayans themselves.

In the process of developing Mayan writers, the ALMG deals

with language and the writing of stories in Mayan languages. As a result, it is the best center for the cultivation of Mayan writers and the promotion of Mayan literature. While there are other Mayan organizations, they don't concentrate on the cultural or literary aspect of Mayan culture.

Many Mayans are also involved in political organizations, such as the United Campesino Committee (CUC), the National Commission of Guatemalan Widows (CONAVIGUA), and the Communities of People in Resistance (CPR). These organizations are made up of the more politicized sectors of the Guatemalan population, including both Mayans and non-Mayans. Their efforts have forced the government to negotiate for change and democracy in Guatemala.

The revitalization of Mayan culture is strongly promoted by the Mayan organizations that include some Native writers. This is what I envisioned when I began to write, that more and more Mayans would write from their particular ethnic backgrounds in an effort to make Mayan culture strong again. The Mayan organizations do not contradict each other but have decided to focus on different issues and to follow different methods and strategies in their struggle for the freedom and survival of Mayan men and women in general. Again, this division shows the need for Mayan culture to revitalize itself in several different aspects. The political, cultural, ethnic, and economic aspects of Mayan life must all be strengthened in order to have a vital Mayan culture in the twenty-first century.

Unfortunately, the political environment in which modern Mayans struggle to reaffirm their identity is still hostile. Nevertheless, with the current government of President Alvaro Arzu, the Mayan population has achieved some freedom of expression and political space. In the cultural aspect, Mayan organizations such as the Consejo de Educación Maya de Guatemala (CEM-G) have managed to organize a national conference on Mayan education in Quetzaltenango with the participation of Guatemalan authorities as well as the elders from some Mayan communities. The conference was intended to find strategies to provide effective education to all Mayans while integrating their values and worldview into their programs of study. Also, as recently as August 1996 the University of Rafael Landivar, in conjunction with other Mayan organizations, organized the First Conference of Mayan Studies in Guatemala, which brought national and international scholars, both Mayan and non-Mayan, together to reorient the field of Mayan studies in Guatemala.

Another important development that has helped Mayan communities to understand and voice their common concerns is the emergence of the bilingual (Spanish-Maya) weekly newspaper *El Regional*. This newspaper originated in Jacaltenango and now covers the whole western region of the country. Information comes from Mayans and non-Mayans and is translated into the Mayan language of the various linguistic communities represented. The newspaper has been a major instrument for gaining an understanding of local history and traditions among Mayans and linking them to the outside world through the local, national, and international news media.

In the political arena, Mayans have been able to present a stronger presence and more visibility as a major ethnic component of the Guatemalan nation. Their insistence on taking part in the peace talks has been fundamental, since no Mayan commission had done so until the end of 1994, when the Assembly of the Civil Society was formed to participate in the peace talks.

It was hoped that Rigoberta Menchu, who had won the Nobel Peace Prize, would be able to influence the peace process, but unfortunately there was little to be done because the two major contending forces, the Guatemalan army and the United Guatemalan National Revolutionary Front (URNG), were both intransigent about signing the peace agreement. But, as mentioned above, Mayans have achieved more visibility in the political life of the nation, so during recent elections for the Guatemalan Congress many Mayan men and women were put forth as candidates by the existing political parties and won seats in Congress. Perhaps the most interesting aspect of the November 1995 presidential election in Guatemala was the emergence of a new political party, the New Guatemalan Democratic Front, organized by the left and the popular movement that included Mayans and non-Mayans. This party did not have a major national impact in the general elections, as had been hoped by the popular movement and opposition leaders.

The Armed Conflict in the Maya Region: The Native Writer's View

Another area that has influenced my work is the armed conflict in Guatemala. As a survivor of a massacre, I was compelled to write a testimony for those who had died and who could not therefore denounce the atrocities to the world.

During early 1982, thousands of Mayans were killed when they were caught in the middle of guerrilla warfare and a scorched-earth counterinsurgency strategy implemented by the Guatemalan army. Some Mayans were involved in the guerrilla movement, of course, but not the majority of Mayans. Despite the refusal of the majority to join the guerrilla movement, the army massacred entire communities, destroying some 440 villages in the Guatemalan highlands. As a result of this policy, a million Guatemalans were uprooted from their homelands and went into internal and external exile.

Because of the urgency of the situation, my academic writing has also centered in part on the political situation affecting the lives of Guatemalans. For example, my doctoral dissertation is on the dynamics of cultural change and the transformation of Mayan culture in the refugee camps in Chiapas, Mexico.[5] In other words, the political situation and my desire to make the refugee situation visible to the world made me write extensively on the refugees. I could have gone somewhere else and written about other indigenous cultures, as most anthropologists do, but I needed to continue with my work in order to contribute to the process of bringing peace and justice for my people. Also, I wanted to demonstrate that Mayans can write stories, folktales, and histories for ourselves. From this perspective, it was interesting that the refugees in Mexico started to organize themselves into artistic groups, whose members then wrote songs and plays as a way of telling people about their collective suffering in the camps.

An interesting aspect of Mayan culture is thus being expressed again. Mayan culture has been able to survive amid violence and repression (the Spanish conquest, colonial rule, modern-day massacres) because it has employed a strategy of collective survival. Mayans have started to recognize the importance of belonging to a common Mayan-based culture, and in this way the various linguistic groups of the Mayan region help each other whenever possible. This policy of collective survival has been depicted in the songs and poems of the refugees themselves who have been singing and writing in their own Mayan languages. For example, in July 1992 I invited Antonio Cota García, a Jakaltek poet and a refugee in Chiapas, to participate in the North American Indian festival called Returning the Gift, where his writings became known.[6] Another example of the creativity of refugees is the work of Manuel Santos, a Jakaltek composer and singer who in 1993 moved to Guatemala City, where he is now producing compact disks.

The life of the Mayan refugees in Chiapas, Mexico, has been difficult. The refugee camps have been relocated many times, and the refugees who have moved to Mexican cities or to other countries have lost several aspects of their culture despite their efforts to maintain links between themselves and the mother culture in Guatemala. The children have grown up in exile and have absorbed elements of Mexican-Ladino culture at the border. Some ten thousand children have been born in refugee camps in Mexico, and they don't know much about Guatemala, which their parents call their homeland.

Because they regret this lack of information about and contact with the expressive culture of their communities through language, dress, festivities, dances, and other traditions, Mayan refugees have started to return to their country of origin—although they too have faced many difficulties in this process because of the armed conflict in Guatemala. The refugees who returned collectively in January 1993 still face insecurities, and their lives are still threatened by the presence of guerrillas and soldiers in the regions where they have decided to build their new communities. This is true for the resettled refugee community of "Aurora, 8 de Octubre" in Xaman in northern Guatemala, where an army incursion resulted in the massacre of eleven men on October 5, 1995. As a result of peace agreements, the demilitarization of the countryside has begun. The army has begun to discontinue the civil patrols in

Mayan communities, where they have persisted since 1982, and guerrilla activity has ceased.

Thus, many of my efforts as an anthropologist and as a writer have been concentrated on the refugee situation. In 1992 I edited a volume called *La Brevísima Relación Testimonial de la Continua Destrucción del Mayab', Guatemala.*[7] This was a group of testimonies collected in the Mayan language and translated into Spanish. My intent was to send a copy to the king of Spain, Juan Carlos de Borbón, just as the defender of the Indians, Fr. Bartolomé de las Casas, bishop of Chiapas, did during early colonial times. The Mayan survivors' descriptions of the torture that has taken place in military barracks are parallel to the cases of torture and dismemberment denounced by las Casas. The comparisons show that five centuries after the first contact, the same crimes continue to be committed against indigenous populations of the Americas.

Will Our Way of Life Be Forgotten?

It is difficult to maintain our cultural traditions when our distinctive way of life is constantly threatened. But as mentioned above, Mayans have managed to make their culture dynamic by accommodating cultural elements from the outside world whenever it has been necessary for their survival. This is the case for modern Mayans who use computers, speak foreign languages, and obtain a higher education from the Western world as instruments for promoting their Mayan culture. Mayan culture, therefore, is being promoted not only on the contemporary intellectual level but also in the more traditional form. For example, in Mayan communities inside Guatemala a very strong movement is seeking to revitalize Mayan culture. The Mayan religion is being revived, and the Ah B'eh, who are diviners (or the Ones Who Show the Path), are again consulting the ancient Mayan calendar.

It is in part modern Mayan writers who have shown the people that Mayan culture is valuable and that we should not be ashamed of it. With our works showing the way for future generations, Mayan culture will surely survive and may again flourish in future *katuns*.[8] Our insistence that Mayan culture and traditions must continue has also helped the elders to recognize that they are not practicing witchcraft but the science of the Mayans embedded in religious and calendrical rituals. As a result, by recognizing the importance of their role, Mayan priests are now coming forth not with fear but with pride in their sacred office.

There are associations of Ah B'eh in most Mayan communities, and they have been reclaiming their right to practice their knowledge and religion freely, without repression or discrimination. For example, in a Congress on Mayan Education in Quetzaltenango, an association of elders insisted that Mayan education should include Mayan values and knowledge in the curriculum. They have also said that the academic cycle should be organized in terms of the Mayan calendar to ensure that Mayan culture is passed down and continued for the benefit of new generations to come. This is a very interesting and important proposal coming from Mayan people themselves—the elders—in an effort to give relevance to Mayan culture and to teach it in the classroom in the way Mayans conceptualize themselves.

As a Mayan writer, I am happy to see that Mayan culture is now being accepted in its modern form. In the past, whenever people talked about Mayan culture they were usually referring to the Classic Mayans, since they did not consider their modern descendants to be the inheritors of that glorious past. Instead, Mayans have been called *indios* and insulted because they did not speak Spanish but only Indian "dialects," which in reality are Mayan languages.[9]

Since the elders are again speaking to the children, modern Mayans must also compromise in order to learn from them and pass on this knowledge to the next generation. We must understand that we too can create from the cultural baggage of our own traditions, and we must be proud of being Mayans. Thus the questions and complaints of the elders in the books of the *Chilam Balam*[10] will be answered positively: Yes, the ancient ways of our ancestors will truly survive in future *katuns*. I repeat, it is the task of the indigenous writer to make sure that the torch continues to burn. The Native writer must show others the road of writing as a way of returning the gift we were given for that purpose. The Native writer, then, has a mission: to keep the torch of his or her culture burning, illuminating the ancestors' path and guiding others to understand why Native cultures are distinct and unique on this earth.

Some Concerns for the Future

As a writer, I recognize that not everything concerning the Mayan culture can be achieved immediately. We have lost much already, such as the reading of hieroglyphs, but we can still learn and recreate from what is left. Unfortunately, the recent Guatemalan conflict—army versus guerrillas—was a major obstacle for the expression of Mayan culture itself. This was a fifty-year-old war, and the indigenous population was caught in the middle. More recently, the war in Chiapas has also decreased the likelihood of a peaceful solution of the armed conflict in the region, and Mayans in Chiapas are in the same condition as their neighbors in Guatemala. They are part of the Mayan cultural base and have likewise suffered discrimination and repression since the Spanish conquest of the early sixteenth century. Mayans of the two regions share the same poverty, landlessness, and a lack of educational opportunities. Historically, Mayan communities in Guatemala and Chiapas have not been seen as full members of their nations but simply as labor forces, and major economic development in the region, including industrial development, has not benefited either of them.

The Zapatista uprising in Chiapas and the guerrilla warfare in Guatemala have been responses to the ill-treatment of the indigenous and poor *campesino* populations. But the armed struggle in both regions will not help to bring peace to the region but simply more reprisals. It is important that the Guatemalan and Mexican governments treat the indigenous Mayan population as integral members of their nations and allow the Mayan people to take part in the proposed industrialization of these regions. In other words, it is very important that Guatemala and Mexico not blame the indigenous populations but provide them with the means for creating a better life within the framework of peace, social justice, and a respect for human rights.

For now, I continue to write in exile because it is still too dangerous to go back to my homeland. Fortunately, I have been able to pursue my career as an anthropologist and have the opportunity to obtain a wider North American audience for my academic and nonacademic writings.

On November 3, 1982, I had to leave my country because it was too dangerous for me to continue working among my people. During that year, the Rios Mont government committed extremely brutal massacres of Mayan communities, and miraculously I survived one of these massacres. By that time, I had finished writing several manuscripts, including *El Q'anil: The Man of Lightning* and *The Bird Who Cleans the World,* and was working on others. This was when a North American writer and journalist, Wallace Kaufman, sent me a letter saying there was interest in publishing a bilingual edition of *El Q'anil* in the United States.

I asked the military officer of the barracks in my town for permission to leave. I told him I was writing educational stories—fables—and I had been given the chance to have a book translated into English and to be published in the United States. This is how I was given permission to travel outside my country for six weeks. The political situation in Guatemala worsened, so I decided to remain in exile to avoid persecution. Meanwhile, I used the time to secure a higher education, obtaining my Ph.D. in anthropology from the University of Connecticut in 1993.

Ten years passed, and finally in January 1993 I went back to Guatemala as a consultant for a film being made on the Mayans of the Kuchumatan region. I accompanied Guatemalan refugees who were returning from Chiapas to Guatemala. Then in December 1993 I was invited by the University of San Carlos Press to attend the presentation and book signing for my book, *Testimony: Death of a Guatemalan Village,* which was finally published in Spanish in my country in 1993. Since then I have continued to visit Guatemala during the summers. I noticed some improvements as a result of the peace process, although there was an increase in common criminality and kidnapping as the date of the signing of the peace accord approached.

As a Mayan writer dealing with the cultural and political situation in my country, I feel more secure writing from exile, although my writings may not be widely known among the Mayan people themselves. One of the major burdens I have to bear is not having the opportunity to write in the Mayan language for a

Mayan audience. I feel, however, that I am bringing some consciousness to the American population on behalf of the Mayan people. I know that the United States is a powerful country, one that can have a positive influence in changing the conditions of violence that Mayans have endured for centuries.

Because of the signing of the peace accord between the Guatemalan government and the Guatemalan National Revolutionary Unity (URNG) on December 29, 1996, there are new hopes for a permanent peace in Guatemala. A pan-Mayan movement is developing from the ashes of the thirty-six-year-old armed conflict, and Mayans are engaged in the revitalization of their culture. We are aware of our cultural patrimonies, and we are focusing on the revival of our institutions and ceremonies. Mayans want to contribute to the construction of a new Guatemalan nation in which Mayan culture is an integral part.

Finally, I am optimistic that the work of the writer has always had a place in history and that writers will continue to work for that end. In this case, Mayan writers should work for the rights of their people to ensure that our message of peace and justice may be passed on to future generations as we enter the new millennium.

Notes

Leslie Marmon Silko

This essay was originally published in *Antaeus,* No. 57 (Autumn 1986). Subsequently, it was the main essay in *Yellow Woman and a Beauty of the Spirit* (New York: Simon & Schuster, 1996).

1. By "ancient people" I mean the last generation or two, which included my great-grandmother, just barely. Their world-view was still uniquely Pueblo.

2. A clan is a social unit that is composed of families who share common ancestors and trace their lineage back to the Emergence where ancestors allied themselves with certain plants, animals, or elements.

3. *Ka'tsinas* are spirit beings who roam the earth and inhabit kachina masks worn in Pueblo ceremonial dances.

4. Chaco Canyon National Historical Park is located in northwest New Mexico, about twenty-four rough road miles southwest of Nageezi on Highway 57.

5. The term *humma-hah* refers to a traditional genre of storytelling at Laguna Pueblo.

6. Laguna and Paguate villages are about forty miles west of Albuquerque in the Laguna Indian Reservation. Highway 279 links the two

villages. Laguna and Zuni Pueblos are the largest of the nineteen contemporary Pueblos (eighteen are in New Mexico, plus the Hopi in Arizona). The Pueblo people are descendants of the Anasazi who lived over a vast area of the Colorado plateau half a millennium and more ago.

7. *The Emergence:* all of the human beings, animals, and life that had been created emerged from the four worlds below, when the earth was habitable. The Migration: the Pueblo people emerged into the Fifth World, but they had already been warned they would have to travel and search to find the place where they were meant to live. The Fifth World is the world we live in today. There are four previous worlds below this world.

8. *Creation:* Tse'itsi'nako, Thought Woman, the Spider, thought about it, and everything she thought came into being. First she thought of three sisters for herself, and they helped her to think of the rest of the Universe, including the Fifth World and the four worlds below.

9. The narratives indicate that the Migration from the north took many years. But the Emergence Place north of Paguate village is only eight miles from Laguna village, the place where the people finally settled. What can it mean that hundreds of years and hundreds of narratives later the Laguna people had traveled but eight miles? Anthropologists attempt to interpret the Emergence and Migration stories literally, with the Pueblo people leaving Chaco Canyon and Mesa Verde to go south to the Rio Grande Valley and to the mountains around Zuni (south of Gallup, New Mexico, on the Arizona border).

Although traditional anthropologists allege otherwise, archaeological evidence will someday place human beings in the Western Hemisphere from the very beginning.

Gloria Bird

1. Jerry Reynolds, "Part I. Indian Writers: Real or Imagined," *Indian Country Today* (Rapid City, S.D.), Lakota Times Section 13, Issue

11, Sept. 8, 1993. See also the series "Indian Writers: Real or Imagined; The Good, the Bad, and the Could Be. Parts II and III."

2. Audre Lorde, "Transformation of Silence into Language and Action," in *Sister Outsider* (Freedom, Calif.: Crossing Press, 1984), 42; and Joy Harjo, "Anchorage," in *She Had Some Horses* (New York: Thunder's Mouth Press, 1983), 15.

3. The Yakama have officially changed the spelling of their name from Yakima to Yakama.

4. These examples are taken from conversations with friends: The uranium mined from Dawn Mine was sold at eight dollars a pound but had a market value of thirty-six dollars a pound. Leased land on the Fort Peck Indian Reservation is leased to a cattle rancher for a dollar an acre a year. The BIA negotiates land, water, and mineral leases for Indian tribes, and underpayment is the rule.

5. Some of the information given in the newspaper article supports the information from the unpublished report cited in this essay, as follows: "Heavy runoff this spring has sent pollutants into small streams that feed the Spokane River and Lake Roosevelt, behind Grand Coulee Dam on the Columbia River. The runoff is contaminated with radiation, heavy metals and sulfuric acid. . . . The mine pits contain a toxic mix of radioactive uranium. . . . The 500 million gallons of contaminated water is too radioactive to be released into waterways. . . . Radiation also emanates from 2.5 million tons of low-grade uranium ore stockpiled on the site" (Associated Press, "Uranium Mine on Reservation Is Leaking," *Wenatchee World,* Okanagon Edition, Northwest Section, May 12, 1997, p. 5).

6. The report entitled "An Investigation into Mining Pollution on the Spokane Indian Reservation" stated that "the unpublished final draft report done by WRD-USGS, received by the BIA–Portland Area Office on December 23, 1983, indicated that in November, 1980, mine drainage had raised the concentrations of most chemical constituents sampled in Blue Creek. Samples taken by the mine operator, USGS, and the BIA since 1980 indicate a gradual decline in surface and ground water quality. Dur-

ing 1984, the mine drainage site was declared a Hazardous Waste Dump by the EPA."

7. After Chief Joseph's eight-year exile in Indian Territory (now Oklahoma), he was not allowed to return to the Wallowa Valley. Instead, he and those people who refused to be Christianized were placed on the Colville Reservation. Other scattered descendants are among the Idaho Nez Perce, Palouse, Umatilla, and Yakama. Others are rumored to be in Canada.

8. Lorde, "Transformation," 45.

Esther G. Belin

1. "surviving in this place called the united states," in *Moving the Image: Independent Asian Pacific American Media Arts,* ed. Russell Leong (Seattle: University of Washington Press, 1991), 245–47.

Roberta J. Hill

1. Crawford Thayer, *Massacre at Bad Axe: An Eyewitness Account of the Black Hawk War of 1832* (self-published, 1984), xxvi, 142–57, 184–85; Arrell Morgan Gibson, *The American Indian: Prehistory to the Present* (Lexington, Mass.: D. C. Heath and Company, 1980), 297–98; and Helen Hornbeck Tanner, *Atlas of Great Lakes Indian History,* The Civilization of the American Indian Series (Norman, Okla.: University of Oklahoma Press, 1987), 151–54.

2. Thayer, *Massacre at Bad Axe,* and Tanner, *Atlas.*

3. Thayer, *Massacre at Bad Axe,* lxi, and Gibson, *The American Indian,* 297.

4. Protests by Indian people like Anishinabe spokesperson Walt Bressette caused the rail shipments of sulfuric acid to stop, at least temporarily. Walt and others who lived there argued that the railroad bridges

were unsafe. For information on these struggles, see Al Gedicks, *The New Resource Wars: Native and Environmental Struggles against Multinational Corporations* (Boston, Mass.: South End Press, 1993).

5. Roberta Hill Whiteman, "A Presence That Found Me Again, Again," in *Philadelphia Flowers* (Duluth, Minn.: Holy Cow! Press, 1996), 106–7.

A. A. Hedge Coke

1. "The Language We Know," in *I Tell You Now: Autobiographical Essays by Native American Writers,* ed. Arnold Krupat and Brian Swann (Lincoln, Nebr.: University of Nebraska Press, 1987).

Daniel David Moses

1. *Coyote City* (Stratford, Ont.: Williams–Wallace, 1990).

2. *The Dreaming Beauty* (Toronto, Ont.: Impulse Magazine, 1989).

3. *Almighty Voice and His Wife* (Stratford, Ont.: Williams–Wallace, 1992).

4. *The Indian Medicine Shows,* two one-act plays (Toronto, Ont.: Exile Editions, 1995). Excerpt reprinted with permission of the author and Exile Editions.

Jeannette C. Armstrong

1. *Gatherings,* vol. 3 (Penticton, B.C.: Theytus Books, 1992).

2. *Gatherings,* vol. 4 (Penticton, B.C.: Theytus Books, 1994).

3. *Breath Tracks* (Stratford, Ont., and Penticton, B.C.: Williams–Wallace/Theytus Books, 1991).

4. Ibid.

5. Ibid.

6. "Frogs Singing," in *Durable Breath,* ed. John E. Smelcer and D. L. Birchfield (Anchorage, Alaska: Salmon Run Press, 1994).

7. *Slash* (Penticton, B.C.: Theytus Books, 1985).

8. Ibid.

9. *All My Relations: An Anthology of Contemporary Canadian Native Fiction,* ed. Thomas King (Toronto: McClelland and Stewart, 1990).

Victor D. Montejo

1. The title of this essay refers to the reading of the hieroglyphs carved in stones that are called stelas.

2. The quetzal is the national currency of Guatemala. During the 1960s and 1970s, the quetzal was at par with the dollar. As of 1997 there were six quetzales to the dollar.

3. Victor D. Montejo, *El Q'anil: The Man of Lightning* (Carrboro, N.C.: Signal Books, 1982, 1984).

4. Victor D. Montejo, *Bird Who Cleans the World and Other Mayan Fables* (Willimantic, Conn.: Curbstone Press, 1991); Victor D. Montejo, *Testimony: Death of a Guatemalan Village* (Willimantic, Conn.: Curbstone Press, 1987).

5. *The Dynamics of Cultural Resistance and Transformations: The Case of Guatemalan-Mayan Refugees in Mexico* (Ph.D. diss., University of Connecticut, Storrs, 1993).

6. The Returning the Gift Festival was a gathering of some five hundred Native American writers for a conference at the University of Oklahoma in July 1992.

7. *Brevísima Relación Testimonial de la Continua Destrucción del Mayab', Guatemala,* ed. Victor D. Montejo (Providence, R.I.: Guatemalan Scholars Network, Providence College, 1992).

8. The *katun* is the Mayan time cycle of twenty years.

9. Twenty-two different Mayan languages are spoken in

Guatemala. All are interrelated, and they stem from the proto-Mayan language.

10. Concerns for the future and the continuation of Mayan knowledge are stated in the *Chilam Balam of Tizimin*. See *The Book of the Jaguar Priest: A Translation of the Book of Chilam Balam of Tizimin,* Maud W. Makemson (New York: Henry Schuman, 1951).

Contributors

Jeannette C. Armstrong, a novelist and poet, is the director of the En'owkin International School of Writing in Penticton, British Columbia, and an Okanagan who is a council member of the Penticton Indian Band in British Columbia. One of Canada's major Native writers, she is a spokesperson for indigenous rights, concerns, and issues, and has addressed assemblies and conferences in Japan, Russia, Switzerland, Germany, New Zealand, the United States, and Canada. Her published works include *Slash* and *Breath Tracks*. A graduate of the University of Victoria with a fine arts degree, she has also been recognized for her visual art works.

Esther G. Belin, has a B.A. from the University of California at Berkeley and an A.A. in creative writing from the Institute of American Indian Arts in Santa Fe. Her poetry has been published in *Neon Pow Wow, Both Sides,* and other publications. One of today's generation of outstanding Native American writers, Ms. Belin is known mainly as a poet, but she is venturing into other forms of writing, including creative nonfiction and fiction, with a recent story in *Voice of the Turtle*. Although raised in a California urban environment, she asserts that the Navajo Nation has always been her homeland.

Gloria Bird, an enrolled member of the Spokane Tribe, is the author of *Full Moon on the Reservation* (which received the Diane Decorah Memorial Award for Poetry in 1993) and *The River of History: Prose Poems.* She edited, with Joy Harjo, *Reinventing the Enemy's Language* and is an associate editor for the *Wicazo Sa Review,* in which some of her critical work has appeared. Ms. Bird lives in Nespelem, Washington.

Allison A. Hedge Coke is a poet, playwright, photographer, and painter, and she has performed on stage and in film. Of mixed-blood heritage, including Tsalagi and Huron, she is a prolific writer, with an M.F.A. in creative writing from Vermont College and an A.F.A. in creative writing from the Institute of American Indian Arts in Santa Fe. Her honors include a Naropa Poetry Prize and a Zora Neale Hurston Award (Naropa Institute M.F.A. summer program awards in 1992 and 1993) and a New Mexico Press Women's Award. Ms. Hedge Coke is the author of *Dog Road Woman* and *The Year of the Rat.*

Roberta J. Hill is an Oneida poet and fiction writer and a scholar who teaches at the University of Wisconsin–Madison. Her major poetry collections include *Star Quilt* and *Philadelphia Flowers,* and her fiction has been published in *That's What She Said* and *Talking Leaves.* Among her awards for writing are a Lila Wallace–Reader's Digest Fund Award and a National Endowment for the Arts Fellowship. Ms. Hill is currently working on an extensive biography of Dr. Lillie Rosa Minoka-Hill, her grandmother.

Victor D. Montejo, a Mayan from Guatemala, obtained his Ph.D. in anthropology from the University of Connecticut, Storrs, in 1993. He has worked extensively with Guatemalan refugees in Chiapas, Mexico, and the United States. His work focuses on the indigenous literatures and oral tradition of the Mayans. His publications include *El Q'anil: The Man of Lightning*; *Testimony: Death of a Guatemalan Village*; *The Bird Who Cleans the World and Other Mayan Fables*; *Brevísima Relación Testimonial de la Continua Destrucción del Mayab', Guatemala*; and *Sculpted Stones*. Dr. Montejo is an assistant professor of Native American Studies at the University of California, Davis.

Daniel David Moses, an outstanding Canadian Native playwright and poet, is a Delaware born at Ohsweken, Ontario, on the Grand River Six Nations lands. His major plays are *Coyote City, Almighty Voice and His Wife,* and *Brebeuf's Ghost. The Moon and Dead Indians* won Vancouver's New Play Centre's Du Maurier Playwrighting Competition, and with its companion piece, *Angel of the Medicine Show* (as *The Indian Medicine Shows*) it won the 1996 James Buller Award for Excellence in Aboriginal Theatre. As a poet he has written *Delicate Bodies* and *The White Line*. He also co-edited *An Anthology of Canadian Native Literature in English*.

Simon J. Ortiz is an Acoma Pueblo author of poetry, short fiction, essays, and a book-length verse narrative on which was based "Surviving Columbus," a 1992 television documentary broadcast by the Public Broadcasting System. Among his works are *The People Shall Continue, From Sand Creek, Woven Stone,* and *After and Before the Lightning*. Besides writing full-time, he conducts writing workshops, presents lectures and storytelling sessions, and gives poetry readings. He has received awards from the National Endowment for the Arts and the Lila Wallace–Reader's Digest Fund.

Leslie Marmon Silko, a novelist, essayist, and poet, is Native America's premier writer. Her most recent book is *Yellow Woman and A Beauty of the Spirit,* following upon *Almanac of the Dead, Ceremony, Storyteller,* and others for which she has achieved national and international acclaim. Over the years she has been recognized with awards and fellowships from the National Endowment for the Arts, the MacArthur Foundation, and the Lila Wallace–Reader's Digest Fund. Originally from Laguna Pueblo, she lives in Tucson, Arizona.

Elizabeth Woody, a poet and prose writer, is a Yakama–Warm Springs–Wasco–Navajo Indian enrolled in the Confederated Tribes of the Reservation at Warm Springs, Oregon. A graduate of Evergreen State College, Ms. Woody taught at the Institute of American Indian Arts in Santa Fe. Presently living in Portland, Oregon, she is with Ecotrust as a program assistant. The author of *Hand into Stone,* which received the American Book Award, *Luminaries of the Humble,* which received the William Stafford Memorial Award from the Pacific Northwest Booksellers Association, and *Seven Hands, Seven Hearts: Prose and Poetry,* she has also published poetry and prose extensively in literary journals, art catalogues, anthologies, and magazines.